brilliant

mindfulness

23/2/15
14/3/15
7.4/15
28/4/15
18/5/15

23/6/15
14/7/15
3/8/15
22/8/15
8/9/15
30/9/15

'If you're looking for an alternative to the frenzy of modern life then this book is essential reading. Cheryl Rezek is the leading light in the movement to make mindfulness accessible to everyone. Her powerful new book is inspiring in a refreshing down-to-earth way that shows her understanding of everyday, real-life challenges. She gives us hope in offering scientifically-based guidance on how mindfulness can help us through the storms and highs of life, as well as increase our quality of life in all areas, from stress and physical illness to emotional distress.'

Ruth Passm   Health, UK

brilliant

mindfulness

How the mindful approach can help you towards a better life

Cheryl A. Rezek

Harlow, England • London • New York • Boston • San Francisco • Toronto • Sydney • Auckland • Singapore • Hong Kong
Tokyo • Seoul • Taipei • New Delhi • Cape Town • São Paulo • Mexico City • Madrid • Amsterdam • Munich • Paris • Milan

PEARSON EDUCATION LIMITED

Edinburgh Gate
Harlow CM20 2JE
Tel: +44 (0) 1279 623623
Fax: +44 (0) 1279 431059
Website: www.pearson.com/uk

First published 2012 (print and electronic)

Pearson Education is not responsible for the content of third-party internet sites.

ISBN: 978-0-273-77413-6 (print)
      978-0-273-78163-9 (PDF)
      978-0-273-78162-2 (ePub)

British Library Cataloguing-in-Publication Data
A catalogue record for this book is available from the British Library

Library of Congress Cataloging-in-Publication Data
A catalog record for this book is available from the Library of Congress

This book makes no claims to act as a cure, preventative measure or treatment
of any condition, nor does it advocate discontinuation of any treatment. The
information in this book is not intended as a substitute for consultation with
healthcare professionals. All use of the material in this book is undertaken solely at
the responsibility of the participant.

10 9 8 7 6 5 4 3 2 1
16 15 14 13 12

Illustrations (except on pages 28 and 29) by Adrian Cartwright at Planet Illustration.

Typeset in Plantin 10/14pt by 3
Printed in Great Britain by Henry Ling Ltd, at the Dorset Press, Dorchester, Dorset

NOTE THAT ALL PAGE CROSS REFERENCES REFER TO THE PRINT
EDITION

To life – I think you forgot to include the manual.

Contents

About the author

Dr Cheryl Rezek is a Consultant Clinical Psychologist who has a long established clinical and academic career working across various fields of mental health. She has headed services, developed treatment programmes and provided consultation, teaching and supervision to a broad set of professionals and organisations as well as to the public.

She has developed an intervention model, Mindfulness-based Multidynamic Therapy (MMT), and she conducts workshops internationally based on it and her bestselling book *Life Happens: Waking up to yourself and your life in a mindful way*. She has a private practice where she provides consultations, supervision, talks, trainings and workshops in addition to authoring work.

www.lifehappens-mindfulness.com

How to use this book[1]

This book is designed to introduce you to the concepts and practices of mindfulness in a straightforward and accessible way. It includes the philosophy of mindfulness, its origins and how it has developed into a mainstream approach that can assist with everyday health and emotional issues. Most importantly, it will give detailed descriptions, suggestions and information on what to do, why to do it and how to move from one step to the next.

The concepts of mindfulness are interspersed with the different practices and exercises that should be used. Mindfulness is an approach to life and can be used without the practices. However, throughout the book, these practices are made available as they are the cornerstone of mindfulness work and are particularly helpful. Using these practices, or exercises, takes the ideas and transfers them into real and practical skills that you can draw on throughout your life. Coupled with these practices are discussions on how you might begin to recognise the effects of your feelings, thoughts and behaviours on your life and whether or not they are interfering or helping you.

You will notice that a CD is provided with this book. The practices on this audio format are also given as written text in each relevant section of the book. The text has been made available so that you can read through the practice and see what it entails. At times, we are reluctant to listen to audio material as we don't know what to expect or we may not necessarily have the equipment available to listen to it. Once you are familiar with it and can see that it doesn't involve anything that

---

1 Footnote numbers in the text refer to the References at the back of the book.

is strange or hypnotic, you will be more willing to make the effort to listen to the relevant section. The written text can also give you the basis of the practice, allowing you time to read and absorb the idea behind it. This can be kept in mind and used wherever you are or with whatever you're doing. For example, the phrases *anchored, balanced and alert* or *use your breath as an anchor* can be said to yourself when you're feeling anxious before an interview or distressed by a situation.

You'll notice on the CD that between each practice title there is a track entitled Gentle Space. This is a 5-minute series of gentle bong sounds that have been included for two reasons. The first is so that one practice doesn't run into the next because if it did you wouldn't know when to stop. The second is that it gives you time to move out of the practice in a smooth and easy way.

The book allows you to become familiar with the concepts associated with mindfulness, such as bringing your attention to this moment in time, being caring towards yourself and mindful breathing. There is a lot of attention paid to breathing as it is a key element in reducing our body's level of stress and arousal, and in rebalancing our internal systems as well as our psychological and emotional states. In addition, it is a core component in mindfulness work. It doesn't involve anything more than your normal breathing process other than paying attention to it and using it in a very beneficial way.

There is a specific section on stress and distress and their medically recognised detrimental effects on our bodies as they are associated with a whole range of situations, such as depression, illness, anxiety, trauma, chronic pain and so forth. Mindfulness practices and a mindful approach to life can help to counteract and reduce some of these negative effects. For this reason, attention has been given to the issue of stress and distress, both physiologically and psychologically.

A chapter can be found that involves gentle body movements. This too is part of mindfulness work as it is important that we reconnect our minds, bodies and breathing. We tend to hold a lot of stress and other emotions within our bodies and these moves will help towards releasing them as well as provide a careful introduction to exercise and body movements.

The latter chapters of the book refer to difficult life situations and how we might manage them using the ideas that have been presented throughout the book. They also look at how you can keep it all on track so that it becomes integrated into your life, piece by piece, over the days, weeks and years to come. There can be important and beneficial shifts that can come about if you continue keeping it in mind and doing the work. There are no quick-fix solutions but there are helpful ideas that can assist and be built upon if you're willing to do the work. This is one of them.

If you are reading this as an eBook, audio MP3 files of the guided mindfulness practices are available to download from www.pearson-books.com/brilliantmindfulness

Living your life is different from being alive.

CHAPTER 1

Jumping off the hamster wheel

n a hurry, rushing about, lacking in time and energy with each day feeling like the last and tomorrow never bringing anything different? Are you feeling trapped on the hamster wheel with no idea of how to stop it without throwing your life into chaos? If this sounds familiar you may be wondering whether this book can be of any use.

Life is difficult much of the time and we don't always know how to manage the various aspects that emerge or get thrown our way. We learn to read

> Life happens to all of us

and do arithmetic, we know how to work computers and drive cars but what we often falter with is the experience and knowledge of how to deal with the tricky and harsh things that occur. These happen not because we are bad people or deserve to suffer but simply because that is what happens in life. Events throw us off balance and challenge our ability to cope.

This is where learning about mindfulness and the practices that come with it can be of invaluable help. It's not only for crises but for all of life, on an everyday basis, and it can be applied to each moment of our lives in one form or another. It builds resources and resilience within you as an individual and it helps to keep life in perspective.

It is tempting to say that mindfulness is taking the West by storm but that would make it sound as if it was something loud and dramatic that swept in, created havoc and then left leaving behind debris and damage. This would give the wrong impression as mindfulness is the exact opposite. It's about managing the storms, both big and small, as well as the sunshine and having a constant at hand that helps you to be resilient within the eye of the storm, mop up some of the damage and feel enabled to enjoy those in-between times of calm and ordinariness.

Mindfulness is fun and serious, easy and hard work, simple and complex.

 **definition**

What is mindfulness?

- bringing awareness to
- whatever is happening
- within you and around you
- in this moment

In essence, it refers to our ability to pay attention to this given moment in an alert and alive manner without distraction or judgement. It focuses on *this* moment in time and what is happening within it rather than simply getting through it. It also encourages you to look at now and not to the past or future.

Multitasking is no longer seen as helpful. It may get you to tick things off your list, but at a cost. Speaking on the phone, driving, listening to the radio, adding items to your shopping list, answering the person in the passenger seat and being annoyed at the driver in front of you simultaneously may sound like a challenge you meet on a daily basis.

You may feel empowered by the challenge, exhausted by the demands of it and more like a wheel-spinning hamster than a person living his or her life. Being pressurised and frantic affects us both emotionally and physically. You go into automatic mode rather than being actively engaged and in control. You get by, day to day, but what may be lacking is feeling that you're involved with your life, that you can really enjoy the ups and not be so shattered by the downs.

 **definition**

Being present in your life is about paying attention to each moment of it.

Everything of interest except ourselves

Is it not surprising that we seek knowledge of stories and beliefs of other places and of vistas of faraway lands yet we so often ignore that which is the most important and unexplained place of all – ourselves? We read autobiographies and biographies of other people's lives but give no time to knowing our own. We even read about fictional characters in novels but are uninterested in the reality of our personal stories, plots and characters. We research annual holidays and new cars for weeks or months in order to get value and reliability but do not do the same for our health and psychological stability that affects us as individuals as well as those around us.

Perhaps it is time to ask ourselves why we have so little interest in ourselves in these areas and why we don't see them as being of much importance and deserving of our time?

Your once-only prized possession

What is your most important or prized possession in the world? For argument's sake, let's take your car as an example. Imagine if you could possess only one car throughout your entire life and that limited repairs could be done over the decades. What would your attitude be towards it? Would you forget to check the oil and water, run it on a flat tyre and never have it serviced?

The answer to all these questions is probably no. If it was chugging as you drove down the street or smoke billowed out from the engine you wouldn't hesitate to take it to the garage. You would take extra care and be alert to any possible defect in the engine so that you could repair any faults as soon as possible and stop further damage occurring. If you didn't, you know you run the risk of it collapsing on you and no longer being of such help in your life.

Whose responsibility is it?

When our physical or psychological health falters we either disregard it or we go to the doctor with the expectation that the physician will prescribe a pill or treatment to make us better. We give responsibility to that person or to the medication to cure us, ease our pain, resolve the problem and restore us to health and wellness. One of the last things we do is say *This is my responsibility – what can I do to help myself?*

This does not suggest that you shouldn't visit your doctor, take your medication or have the required surgery. In fact, it is the very opposite of that. What it does suggest is that you shift the belief that something outside of you is always responsible for your physical and mental health, your happiness and welfare, and then engage with all possible and appropriate means that can alleviate the pain, reduce your blood pressure, decrease your anxiety, lift your depression or help you manage the drop in quality of life from illness, distress or poor self-care.

Questionnaire

Do you have thoughts running through your head before you're even fully awake?

Do you rush out of bed in the mornings?

Do you miss breakfast or gobble it down?

Do you do more than one task at a time, such as eat your toast while getting dressed, speak on the phone while driving, watch TV and have an important conversation?

Have you ever started doing one thing and then forgotten to finish it?

Have you looked back on something good that happened and realised how little you were able to appreciate it or really enjoy it to its fullest?

Does it feel as if your life is moving ahead with or without you?

If you've answered yes to any of these questions then you're probably like most of us - in a rush and on the go, forgetting sometimes where we are and why we're here.

Knowing you have a choice helps you to feel more in control

We all know what it is like when we speak to someone and that person is distracted even if they are sitting still and nodding. You sense it and are aware that they're preoccupied and not really listening to you, nor respecting your being there. It isn't a nice feeling and yet we constantly do that to ourselves. We tend not to listen to ourselves, to our distress, fears or needs and so we can't give ourselves the respect and care that we ought to. We nod at our own voice that says we really need to drink less, lower our stress levels, show more love to our partners, be less aggressive in our cars or address our diabetes and hypertension in a more serious way. There are many more examples so why not give a moment's thought to one or two that you dismiss.

> You are your life – they are not two separate things

When we recognise that we have an option as to how we conduct our lives and the choices we make then we start to feel more in control of what happens to us. We cannot know what tomorrow, next week or next year will bring. We can't even know what will come within the next few seconds of our lives. This sense of unpredictability can motivate us to use and be present within this one moment where we do have knowledge and certainty. We can only live this moment if we acknowledge its existence for all that it is and we can do this by noticing it, knowing it is here and deciding how we are going to be within it. In other words, this stress is mine so will I be rude or panic-struck or will I focus on something that can reduce it? Will you reach for another drink when the depression or loneliness feels so intense or will you begin to work with it? Do you flood yourself with self-hate and anger when life is harsh or do you step back and acknowledge how much it hurts but learn to manage it in a less destructive way?

The importance of self

When you can admit to yourself that you are your own responsibility then you can take back your control and establish your importance in your own life. This allows you to recognise that you are a once-only possession that deserves to be taken care of and given time. This doesn't refer to the overdeveloped sense of importance and ego that is encouraged in the world at present – that *I, me, myself* attitude where we boost selfishness and a sense of entitlement or where we revere badly behaved celebrities and look to them as role-models.

We envy those with possessions and money, not those who generate kindness and genuine concern, we watch humiliating reality TV shows and buy gossip magazines, we applaud brash and crude behaviour but seldom do we think about how important it is for us to be watching the reality show of our own lives and what internal destruction and gossip takes place in our heads about our failings, misdemeanours and behaviours. This isn't a statement on the moral state of the world but on how our focus has turned inwards towards entitlement – *I want, I deserve* – or outwards towards the titillating behaviour of celebrities. What we seem to have overlooked is the importance of looking at ourselves and being with ourselves, even if it feels uneasy.

Being mindful

We live in a world where the expectation is that life should be perfect and without suffering, struggle or loss. This myth places us in a state of dissatisfaction as we believe that somehow we have failed if our lives are difficult or we go through hard times.

We are busy, preoccupied and distracted and we complain of needing more time, more hands, more money and more relaxation. Even before we are fully awake we start to think of the day's requirements and forget that the day belongs to us rather than us to our list of demands.

We eat more but feel less full, we buy more but feel less secure and satisfied, we know more through education and technology but feel more isolated, depressed and have a greater sense of discontent. It appears that the more we have, in terms of availability and access, the less happiness we feel. The levels of anxiety, depression, stress, sleep problems, distress, loneliness and dissatisfaction are at an all-time high despite what we have. The reason for this may be down to the lack of quality we feel within ourselves.

Being mindful shifts the emphasis and offers an alternative to the rush and frenzy of modern life by suggesting that we can pursue nothing, live in the present and still achieve all that we want. This seems contradictory as we are taught to be goal-orientated and fixed on how to get it. Mindfulness suggests that we can learn to respond to our needs and desires in a thoughtful and considered way rather than grasping at life and experiences in a reactive and thoughtless manner.

We are seldom taught to manage life issues and so feel ill-equipped to deal with them. For example, when something good happens we're encouraged to blur it with a celebratory drink rather than savour the wonderful moment. When something painful happens, we are taught to hide the depth or intensity of our feelings, to put on a brave face and to get on with life. Neither is wrong but the emphasis is on hiding our feelings or diluting them rather than staying with them, knowing that we can deal with them.

Being human means that we encounter a whole range of events, feelings, thoughts and experiences that include change, joy, distress, pleasure, illness, fear, suffering, calm, anxiety, anger and grief, amongst others. The difference that mindfulness can make is that it helps us to experience the *now* exactly as it is including all our senses, thoughts, desires, emotions and feelings. We begin to *notice* what is happening rather than react, intellectualise, dismiss or deny it.

There is probably some minor annoyance that you experience every day - noise, traffic, queues, rudeness, incompetence etc.

How do you react to these events at all levels?

- What thoughts go through your head?
- What emotions surge up?
- What physical response is there in your body?
- What action do you take?

Do you lash out, withdraw, shout, blame yourself or others, get into a bad mood for the rest of the day, develop a headache, have a drink, drag on a cigarette, take it out on someone else, cry or feel sick?

Life happens now

Life is going to happen regardless of our moods or fears. Being mindful helps us to see clearly and feel fully the ever-changing movement of life. We often wish we could change the past or predict the future but all that we have is the present. Whereas we can't change the present in all ways, what we do have control over is how we deal with it within this very moment. It is this that gives us choice – do we lash out or contain our anger, do we fight against the pain of reality or do we work with it and see it within the context of life being a moving and changing experience, even if we wish it could be fixed and immoveable?

The word mindful is now frequently seen and heard in many areas whether in the media or by friends and colleagues. The meaning of it is to be aware, to pay attention to something. This comes from the concept of mindfulness that is a practice or way of being that originates from the Buddhist philosophy.

Crossing the Himalayas

In the context of Buddhism, it started in India with the prince who left his insulated royal life in order to seek knowledge of what truths lay outside the palace walls about life, suffering and enlightenment. He spent many years seeking this wisdom, coming to the conclusion that life is a series of impermanent events and feelings, that it is transient and that our attachment to items and people is what causes suffering. Amongst many other beliefs and insights that he developed and taught, one that came to the attention of the western world was mindfulness. In essence, mindfulness is the capacity we all hold to focus our attention on the present moment, right here right now, and to keep it focused for whatever is happening, whether pleasant or difficult.

Over two and a half thousand years ago, the teacher who became known as Buddha (which means enlightenment) shared his knowledge with those who were interested. They, in turn, shared their experiences and Buddhism became a well-established philosophy by which to live one's life. Buddha never wanted, or aimed for, his teachings to be regarded as a religion of any kind. For him, it was a way of setting out to understand and live life rather than to have any deity status attached to him or his teachings. Buddhism, in real terms, is not a religion and it is the doing of generations in eastern countries over the centuries that at times gives it such a status.

Many individuals from the western world have sought out the ideals and tenets of Buddhism either through spending time in monasteries or in teaching communities where the rules are strict and meditation practice is expected to be undertaken for long stretches of time. Some have become monks and remained there, others returned to the West as monks or have simply come back to their homes of origin and continued with their beliefs and practices as part of their ordinary western lifestyles.

There is no mystery attached to Buddhism but perhaps it has been categorised as such because we tend to associate it with chanting, incense and loincloths. We only see orange-clothed men with bowls, levitating yogis or people sitting cross-legged in silence for many hours at a time. What we don't get to see is the wisdom of the teachings. Buddhist principles and values are no different from other more familiar ones that are evident in Christianity, Judaism or the Muslim faith. At the centre of all are principles of kindness, truth, leading a good and decent life, care and compassion for others and how to conduct ourselves within the world. They may differ in ideas of structure, hierarchy and eternity but they mostly encourage people to live decent lives in a difficult world.

Developing new approaches

Those western individuals who found their way back to their lands of origin didn't forget the important lessons and practices they had found, either in the East or perhaps with like-minded people at home. Where many preferred to continue these practices and lifestyles in a more purist way, others began to see that certain aspects of Buddhism could be translated into a programme or structure that could be of enormous benefit to people who had no interest in Buddhism as such.

This idea began to take shape in 1979 in a hospital setting in Boston at the University of Massachusetts with Jon Kabat-Zinn, a molecular biologist and keen meditator. He and colleagues believed that a specific practice referred to as mindfulness meditation, coupled with certain principles such as compassion and non-critical observation and with mindful body movements, could provide assistance to those in distress.

The hospital had many patients suffering from illness, stress and distress who appeared to need additional intervention to that provided by medicine, not as a replacement but as something that could help them manage their situations rather than cure them.

Kabat-Zinn and his colleagues put together a programme called Mindfulness-Based Stress Reduction (MBSR) which was based on Buddhist practices that were adapted to a western audience. The medical staff of the hospital were eager, if sceptical at first, to have an additional referral source for suitable patients and so the beginnings of a now internationally recognised programme were laid down. The programme found appeal as it was secular and readily understood. However, perhaps its greatest appeal was that it provided concepts and practical tools that could be used by those in distress or having difficulty dealing with their life situations. Overall, although the original programme has had some expected alterations made to it, the core components and philosophy have remained much the same.

Mindfulness-based work is now more prominent and sought after than ever before due to the scientific evidence that is being gathered to support its claims. The roots of all mindfulness-based work first belong to those original Buddhist concepts and practices from centuries ago and, more recently, to the westernised programme developed by those at the University of Massachusetts.

What can mindfulness do for you?

- Reduce stress, anxiety and depression – even shyness and anger.
- Provide health benefits such as decrease hypertension, improve the immune system and lessen psoriasis.

- Improve quality of life when ill with cancer or other conditions.
- Assist with the management of chronic pain, including arthritis, acute pain and even with childbirth.
- Assist with addictions, trauma and severe life disruptions.
- Assist with quality of sleep.
- Improve concentration and attention (in adults and children).
- Assist with parenting skills.
- Provide a balanced approach to life at a personal and professional level.
- Develop and improve resilience and skills to manage life.

A taste of mindfulness

- When you're in the shower slow down completely and actually feel the sensation of the drops of water hitting your skin. Open your mouth and allow the water to enter your mouth or put your tongue out and notice the drops landing on it, the taste of the water, the water pouring over your lips and chin.

> Mindfulness is different from what we have come to expect in life

- Take a piece of chocolate, some yoghurt or anything that isn't too difficult to chew. Eat it as normal. Now take a second helping and bring all of your attention to the sensation in your mouth. Let the food remain in your mouth without chewing or swallowing, then very slowly begin to chew. Notice the flavour, where in your mouth you can taste it, is it sweet or salty, rough or smooth? Is it difficult to slow down your rate of chewing, can you control your urge to swallow?

- Stand, or stay sitting, wherever you are and be very still. Bring your attention to the sounds that are around you. Are they loud or soft, close or far away, gentle or jarring? Do you recognise them, remember hearing them a few minutes ago or are they new to your awareness? Are there birds singing or cars driving by, are fingers hitting a keyboard or are people chatting?

The difference between relaxation and meditation

Mindfulness meditation or mindful awareness is very different from relaxation. The main issue is that of intent. In relaxation one looks to unwind and to *switch off*. Meditation is about *switching on* to yourself. It's about becoming alert to what is happening within your mind, body and self as well as your interaction with the world around you in the present moment.

Mindfulness works to bring about an intentional awareness to you, about you, within you and for you. It encourages you to know the situation, bring awareness of it into consciousness and to then decide how you might like to respond. For example, if you're feeling anxious you can bring your focus to your anxiety, recognise it and either be annoyed or angry that you're feeling this way and go deeper into the state of anxiety or you can acknowledge it, focus on your breathing and allow the feeling to dissipate without being harsh or cruel to yourself.

You will read more about this throughout the book and be given ways to develop this approach.

brilliant suggestion

Find somewhere where you won't be interrupted and listen to a short piece of music. Give all of your attention to it, becoming aware of the melody, the variety of instruments, the movement of the sounds, the very first and last notes.

More about mindfulness

Mindfulness is about being present in the present. That may sound obvious but we have a tendency to be here in body but somewhere else in our heads. Mindfulness helps us to live within this moment in an alert and aware state for whatever is happening. It is not about emptying the mind. Rather, it is about becoming aware of all that is happening within yourself, regardless of what it is.

Many people who experience issues such as stress, illness, cancer, anger, trauma, emotional distress or chronic pain have a tendency to lose the belief that they can shift their lives into a more manageable state[53]. Mindfulness helps you to notice and accept the many states of emotion and physical sensations that we can experience whether they are pleasant or distressing. It not only helps with the difficult aspects of life but it can also provide a place of support and stability for all times. At the centre of it is our approach to life and our breathing. The idea of how we can use our breathing as an anchor in order to accept and manage our lives may sound strange but remember – *if we aren't breathing we aren't living.*

Mindfulness is not a treatment where you can expect some form of cure. It is a way of being, an approach to life. It can be incorporated into your life at every moment and in so doing it can bring about shifts and changes. It can be nurtured and developed, not purchased or injected.

The fact that one cannot swallow a pill and become mindful may be disappointing to some as we all look for magic wands to make us happy, well, rich and content. The truth is, there are no magic wands and not even pills or promised cures turn out to be as magical as they sound.

As with all things in life, some come easy and others require attention and perseverance. Developing a mindful way of going about your life, and using the practices that help you to take a step into being involved with your life rather than simply getting through it, day by day, struggle by struggle, may offer something different from what is usually advertised. The great advantage of it is that even though it isn't instant and doesn't claim to be a cure-all it is entirely within your control and the more you do it the more it transforms your life.

The simple things in life

Do one activity in your day, each day, in a focused and attentive manner. Examples of activities are washing your hands, drinking a cup of tea, washing dishes, walking to the car, getting dressed or undressed, chopping vegetables and watering the garden.

Give the activity your complete attention.

● Notice the touch, feel, smell, sound and taste of it.

● Observe where your mind goes and the distractions to which you respond.

● Be aware of your breathing and the changes that occur as you focus on the task.

brilliant example

John was a young man with the world at his feet. He was working, building a career for himself, earning good money and generally living life with a carefree and optimistic attitude. He never thought about himself in any serious way and he usually found anything along those lines irrelevant.

Within moments his life changed. He had a heart attack and nearly died. He stopped breathing on two separate occasions and was revived and treated and he soon began to make good progress. A few months later he began to lose interest in life. He became increasingly anxious and had difficulty breathing, he lost his confidence, he became more isolated and he started to drink in order to numb his feelings. He gradually became more and more depressed and hopeless, reaching the point of wanting to end his life.

He came across mindfulness work through a friend who asked him to give it a try. At first he was sceptical and embarrassed as he felt ashamed of his feelings. After all, he had been clinically dead and was brought back to life so he ought to be grateful and elated. He was uneasy about trying something that sounded fluffy and he felt too depressed to believe that anything could help.

He reluctantly started to read up on the topic and decided to try a few of the practices. He found it difficult to concentrate but he noticed that when he actually did a practice he would feel different. Over time, and with an increase in his belief that mindfulness could work for him, he gradually learnt more about himself as well as how to manage his feelings and behaviour. His anxiety attacks began to lessen, his depression started to ease and most importantly, he began to take on board the idea that even though life can change at any time he now had a more stable and resilient way of managing his feelings and dealing with life.

This chapter has given you an overview of mindfulness, its origins and developments and how it might be relevant to your life. The following chapter will look at the research that is emerging on the use of mindfulness as well as on the issues of distress and stress, which you'll remember were mentioned in the *How to use this book* section.

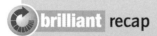 **recap**

- Mindfulness is an approach to life.
- It involves developing a way of being as well as practices.
- It is not a cure or magic wand.
- Everyone can develop and use it, sceptics included.
- If you can breathe in and out then you can start the work.
- It is not relaxation nor does it involve an altered state of mind.
- It is about waking up to your life.

Don't do the same thing and expect a different result.
If you put your hand on a hot stove it's going to get
you burned. If you don't want your hand to get burned,
don't put it on the hot stove.

CHAPTER 2

From mountain tops to the laboratory: the science of stress and mindfulness

W e all know what it is like being stressed – we're tense, distracted, less patient and generally feel like a rubber band being pulled in different directions. What we don't always realise is the amount of damage it can cause our bodies and our minds.

Did you know that in the UK:

- stress is the second biggest cause of long-term absence from work after back pain and
- depression and anxiety are the most common stress-related complaints seen by doctors?

Its effects are so widespread and harmful that clinicians are now focusing on ways of helping people lessen their stress levels in more structured ways. Mindfulness has been identified by clinicians as key to reducing stress – in fact, the original mindfulness-based stress reduction programme was developed with precisely this in mind. Its success and usefulness, which is outlined below, is evidence of how very effective mindfulness work is in lowering stress, improving health and quality of life, increasing areas of mental functioning and shifting behaviour.

The evidence: how mindfulness can help with stress, depression, illness and more

Buddhist philosophy recognises that with life comes suffering and that mindfulness is an effective way with which we can manage suffering and our life issues. Mindfulness meditation has caught the eye of neuroscientists who are using some of the most advanced equipment available (such as fMRI scans) to measure and detect changes in the brain structure of individuals who use mindful practices and compare them to people who don't or who are new to them. This gives us extraordinary proof of how effective it can be. Other research is also extremely valuable as it too shows how useful it is in people's lives across many different areas. The positive results seen below are evidence of what can come about from using the mindfulness practices in this book on an ongoing basis.

- **Stress/Distress.** It decreases stress, increases positive emotions and quality of life[2] and decreases the secretion of the stress hormone, cortisol[3].

- **Anxiety.** It decreases anxiety[4, 5] and feelings of panic[6] as well as depression and irritability[7].

- **Mood.** It helps to lift our mood and to keep our emotions more balanced[8, 9] as well as lessen our negative emotions[8]. It even helps us to ruminate less[10, 11, 12], it decreases symptoms of depression[12] and it increases overall wellbeing. It helps to prevent relapse of depression[13] and assists with traumatic memories and other symptoms of trauma[14, 15, 16].

- **Wellbeing.** It improves our wellbeing[17, 18] and allows us to be more attuned to ourselves[18, 19].

- **Relationships.** It can improve couples' relationship satisfaction, levels of closeness and acceptance of each other[20] as well as help with sexual dysfunction[21, 22].

- **Addictions.** It helps prevent relapse in addiction[23, 24] and cravings[25] as well as with depression that can occur in substance misuse[26]. It can also help when trying to stop smoking [27] and with binge eating[28].

- **Medical conditions.** It reduces the detrimental effects of psoriasis[30] and helps in weight and food management[28]. It can improve sleep quality and lessen sleep interfering processes such as worrying[31, 32]. It enhances immune function[9, 33, 34] in healthy people as well as in those with HIV/AIDS[33, 34] and cancer[35, 36]. It helps with chronic lower back pain[29, 37], symptoms associated with fibromyalgia[29, 38, 39], multiple sclerosis, rheumatoid arthritis[29, 40], premenstrual syndrome[29], type II diabetes[29], cardiovascular disease[41] and asthma[52]. In cancer patients it helps to reduce stress, pain, anxiety[42], depression and cancer-related fatigue[43, 44] in addition to improving sleep[45, 46], quality of life[35] and a sense of happiness[42].

- **The brain.** Mindfulness meditation increases grey matter in areas of the brain that are associated with recognising internal sensations, thoughts and emotional feelings[47, 48, 49], reasoning and decision making, improved attention[3, 50], memory, reaction times and mental and physical stamina[25, 26], and with controlling our emotions and behaviour[3, 25, 51].

These studies show that mindfulness meditation can increase your health, wellbeing and quality of life as well as help build a fit, resilient and resourceful mind for those times when your life is stressful and a struggle.

As stress is linked to so many physical and psychological conditions, it is essential to understand what happens when you are stressed so that you can recognise why and how mindfulness work can help you manage these situations.

Below is a checklist – which do you think apply to you?

- shortness of breath or shallow breathing
- palpitations
- disturbed sleep
- headaches or stomach aches
- agitation or restlessness
- feeling withdrawn
- less enthusiasm about life
- a drop in your work performance
- loss of interest in sex or impotence
- anxiety or depression
- change in mood or uncharacteristic behaviours, such as aggression or risk taking
- increased use of alcohol or drugs, including prescription, over the counter or illicit drugs

You may be surprised to read that all of these are signs of stress, so if you ticked one or more it may be worth thinking about your stress levels and what you can do about them. The mindfulness programme in this book will help to reduce the negative impact associated with a range of health and psychological areas and life difficulties as they all create the same stress-related response within us, which is described below. Mindfulness will also help you to develop improved ways of dealing with these life issues so that the stress created by them can be managed in a beneficial way.

The stress response

The reaction in our bodies to stress isn't only about feeling tense but it happens when there are other issues at hand. We become stressed for a variety of reasons such as work overload, relationship difficulties, financial worries, poor sleep or being a carer. Having an illness such as cancer, hypertension, asthma or diabetes can cause stress as can being in chronic pain from back pain or arthritis. We often forget that stress can come about from emotional states like being anxious, depressed, angry or fearful or be a result of trauma or bad memories. Our beliefs and expectations of ourselves and life can also lead to stress and examples of these are being perfectionist, fearing criticism, feeling inadequate or having poor self-esteem.

> Stress and distress are psychological states that are translated into a physical reaction

We may not be directly aware of feeling stressed but our bodies are reacting and interacting with our emotional states on an ongoing basis. We tend to think of stress as being a physical response and forget that it first starts in our head and this then triggers a chain reaction in our bodies.

Our minds and bodies are geared towards survival because this basic and powerful instinct allows us to continue existing not only at this moment but as a species. Consequently, our survival radar is extremely sensitive so that we can detect the smallest piece of information that might alert us to any danger. It is similar to how quickly a bird will react to the smallest movement or sound even when we cannot see or hear it.

In humans, when we sense that danger may be about our bodies automatically go into a state of alertness usually before we have recognised any threat. For example, when we hear a loud or unexpected noise, like a car backfiring or a tray falling on tiles, we react long before we actually know what has caused it and whether or not it is a threat to us.

When we get stressed about life issues or through emotional and physical conditions our mind doesn't recognise that we aren't in actual physical danger but it reacts as if there is a real threat. For example, even though you know that being late for an appointment or being in chronic pain isn't life-threatening the survival system in your brain doesn't, so it gets ready to help protect you. One of three things can happen: you get ready to fight, to run (flight) or you shut down and become unable to move (freeze).

> Our bodies can't distinguish between psychological and physical danger so they react to any potential threat in the same way

Go mode

When you need to fight or run, the remarkable design of your brain sets about getting your body into the *go mode* by activating the sympathetic system (which is part of your autonomic nervous system).

Your survival radar thinks you are in danger so it sets off your alarm system and releases what we refer to as the stress hormones, which are mostly cortisol and adrenaline. Your body organs not needed for immediate survival are slowed down so that energy can be focused on increasing your heart and breathing rates as well as your arm and leg muscles. By this stage your body is in a heightened state of arousal and you are on high alert so you can fight the lion or run like crazy[1]. However, your body responds not only to real threats, such as a lion jumping out at you, but also to what it *thinks* is a danger even if you know it isn't one. What happens is that your body interprets the situation as a potential threat to your safety (this is referred to as a perceived danger) and reacts as though you are under threat. Examples of this are getting agitated in a traffic jam, working under too much pressure or feeling strong emotions when in pain or distressed. You know these situations aren't dangerous but nevertheless they still activate the stress response as your mind tells your body that you are under strain and may need to be on high alert.

The third option, in addition to flight or fight, is when people are overwhelmed by fear and are unable to move. They become like a rabbit in headlights and are psychologically and/or physically immobilised. Alternatively, they may become emotionally detached and seem distant. This response may have developed as a form of protection in past situations, such as when there was ongoing abuse or fear and the safest option was to not react.

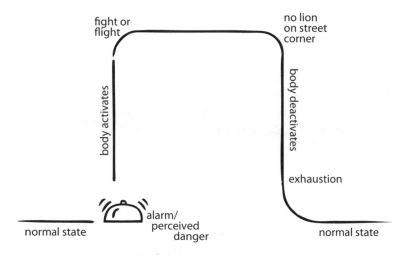

Body's response to stress

Stop mode

When you have fought off the lion, run to safety or eased away from the freeze position your body needs to return to a normal state. The stop mode is when the brakes are put on (by the counterpart of the sympathetic system, the parasympathetic system) so that your high alert state can be slowed down and your body brought back down to a balanced level.

While you were in the *go mode*, energy was redirected from the digestive system, which meant that the vital tasks of digestion, absorption, excretion and other essential functions that are needed for cell growth and for producing your body's energy sources had been put on hold. One area that would need that energy is your immune system which is key for fighting off bacteria and viruses, even early cancer cells, and in helping to repair damaged tissues. This reaction to stress also affects the part of the brain that allows for clear thinking and sleep, so if you get stressed too often it can interfere with your sleep, and if you don't sleep well your immune system can't fight infections and repair your body[1].

Effects of stress and distress

The problem comes in when the stress response is over-activated. This leads to your body going into *go mode* when it doesn't need to be in it but your body still releases the stress hormones. When they are released too often your body gets confused and overworked so it produces too little or too much of them when they are actually needed. They are powerful hormones so too much of them, too often, can put strain and wear on your organs and interfere with your body's functions. It's like sitting in your stationary car and repeatedly revving it and then putting your foot on the brake. The result is that you waste petrol and wear out the parts for no reason as you aren't driving the car to go anywhere.

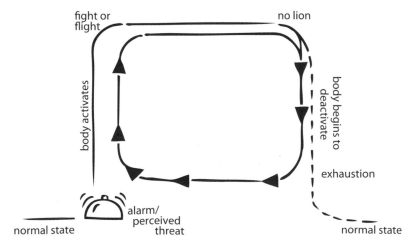

Body's response to chronic/ongoing stress

With stress, our organ and memory cells can get damaged, our thinking is affected and we tend to get more fat deposits around our waist which increases our risk of heart disease. Stress is also implicated in irritable bowel syndrome, ageing, depression, hypertension (high blood pressure), rheumatoid arthritis, diabetes, cancer, pain conditions, such as fibromyalgia, sleep, infertility, impotence, loss of libido, sexual and relationship difficulties, work performance, poor concentration and a decrease in quality of life.

By this stage, there is probably little doubt in your mind about the negative effects of stress on your body and how your mind and body react to each other. So, stress, tension, depression, anxiety, family demands, financial or relationship concerns and work pressure are not only emotional states but ones that can also impact on your physical health as they kick-start the stress response.

brilliant insight

You can't de-stress or cope with distress if you don't acknowledge that they are there and how they affect you. Once you recognise their impact you can then think about what to do.

brilliant example

Gill expected her life to turn out the way it had. She had three children, a caring husband, a nice house and a great job. On the surface it all seemed wonderful except for her need to be seen as perfect. Her life was good but the family commitments were high and her work demands never-ending. Life was great except that she felt like a failure, like a zombie rushing to meet one demand after the next. Her sleep was restless and her heart often pounded in her chest but what else could she expect when she had so many things on her mind? Her children were lovely, but she didn't really have the time to chat to them about their day as she was busy, nor could she actually watch them perform at sport as she was usually sitting in the car checking her list of things to do and talking on the phone. What she couldn't understand was why she felt miserable and strung out when she had it all.

This underlying feeling of emptiness and flatness began to weigh heavily on her. Her moods were up and down, she wasn't feeling able to cope and she felt sick much of the time. A visit to her doctor confirmed that her blood pressure was raised, her stomach pains seemed to have no physical cause and her tiredness wasn't due to illness or anaemia. What Gill was suffering from was stress.

At first she was appalled to hear that she might be so weak as to be suffering from stress. She thought it must be hormonal or due to an underlying but missed illness. She had everything so how could she be stressed? Mindfulness work was mentioned to her by a health professional. It took a fair amount of time and perseverance for her to recognise that beneath her good life lay a person who was self-critical and who feared failure, someone who tended to dismiss her real feelings of fear and anger, a person who held it all in and did what she expected of herself and what others came to expect of her too.

It was through her gradually, albeit reluctantly at times, noticing what she was doing that she could see past her layers of protection and recognise her high expectations, her harsh and critical view of herself and how she was so fixed on achievement. She came to see that she was being a good practical mother and wife but not an engaged one and how her children were growing up right before her eyes but she was more involved with her to-do list than the daily events of their lives. She was sad to realise that she could see them run around on the sports field but not notice the excitement in their eyes when they managed a difficult manoeuvre.

She began to recognise the value of self-care and of slowing down so that she could experience what was happening in her everyday life rather than rushing through it at high speed. Her blood pressure began to normalise, her stomach aches disappeared, her sleep was more restful and even when she was angry with one of her children for losing an expensive blazer, her husband for leaving the car without petrol and deeply saddened when her mother died sooner than expected, she could step aside from her old responses and manage her feelings and reactions in a way that took care of her.

Stress can be damaging to us both physically and psychologically. It is easy to dismiss the signs of stress and distress, believing they are normal or will disappear when a situation passes but this attitude may not be the most helpful. It is better to acknowledge what is happening and to use mindfulness as a means of dealing with it, so the following chapter will introduce you to some mindful practices that you can use.

brilliant recap

- Distress and stress are psychological states that can also lead to physical conditions.

- They interfere with your health and emotional wellbeing.

- Stress is linked to a number of physical conditions.

- Mindfulness can help to regulate your stress, distress, mood, pain, fear, eating, addictions and illnesses.

- It can assist in improving your quality of life and your general wellbeing and happiness.

No matter where we go we are always there.

CHAPTER 3

The mind–body connection

We looked at how the mind and body interact with each other in the previous chapter and how the stress response is activated even when we don't realise it. Here we will discuss the mind–body relationship in more detail and link it to the important and life-giving issue of our breathing. You may be wondering how this has any relevance to mindfulness but you'll soon come to see that being aware of your breathing is the central point of mindfulness work as the way in which we breathe can help lower our levels of emotional and physical stress and refocus our attention on that part of ourselves that is stable and resilient.

Mind and body

The scientific and medical fields tended to view the mind and the body as separate entities for many centuries and this gave rise to the belief that although these two parts were within one individual they were not strongly interconnected in terms of emotions or thoughts influencing the functioning of the body. However, there was some awareness that our bodies' mechanisms and chemicals could impact on our moods, such as with dopamine (it makes us feel good) or serotonin (it regulates our mood). The reference was mostly to the brain's processing ability and its vital function of sending and receiving messages to and from the rest of the body in order for us to breathe, have our hearts pump at regular intervals, develop sexually at puberty and so forth. What was not emphasised was that the mind (that thinking/feeling/emotional part of us) could exert enormous influence over our physical bodies and brains. In many ways, the mind's influence on the body, both positive and disruptive, was regarded as being of secondary importance by scientists.

In more recent years, a shift has taken place which is giving a much needed awareness to the fact that we are mind *and* body, not mind *or* body, and that we are *one* unit that is interconnected at every level[53]. Our brain is the physical structure that sends messages to the organs and systems to generate responses and to process information. Our mind is the part that contains our emotions, feelings and thoughts and our bodies are the organs and systems that allow us to present as a human being. These components are intertwined and interact in a sophisticated and complex manner.

Breathing

At the centre of mindfulness practices are focusing and breathing. This may sound new age but it's more old age considering how many centuries such practices have actively been in place.

The key issue is that if we aren't breathing we aren't living. It's as simple and factual as that. We hear of people on life-support machines and such machines are often breathing machines. Consequently, it makes sense to focus on one of the fundamentals of our existence. If it keeps us alive then it may be worth getting past the idea that paying attention to it is silly or alternative and recognise its tremendous importance.

We shouldn't forget just how portable our internal breathing apparatus is, so that too is an advantage as we can engage with it wherever we are, whenever we wish to. We can be sitting on the bus, working on the car, involved in a high-level meeting or giving birth. There is no instance where we leave our breath at home or forget it at the office, except when we're dead.

Breathing life into your life

Mindfulness is an approach to life, a way of engaging with yourself and the world around you in an alert and awake manner. This is a capacity we have from birth, but rather than having it nurtured and developed we often have it curtailed and restricted. There are many demands made on us as we move from infancy to adulthood, some of which distract us from what is happening within us at this very moment.

We are taught to look at the past, to speculate on the future and to use our intellect and cognitive thinking rather than our instinctual awareness and responses. We are judged by our critical thinking and analytic skills, by the evidence we can produce to support an argument and by our monetary or material acquisitions. How often do we know of the charity worker who takes food to the poor or risks his or her life to save people in floods or children from being trafficked? On the other hand, how easy is it to not know of the latest scandal in sport or a celebrity's most recent episode of bad behaviour?

A practice is an exercise

There is a wide range of practices with which you can get involved. The word practice is similar to that of exercise. *Exercise* is often associated with a keep fit regime whereas *practice* is more to do with a routine, a way of carrying out a procedure. The important issue is that you don't get put off by the word *practice* as its meaning is similar to that of training, task or procedure.

The following are exercises or practices that can help you to develop awareness and to focus attention on different aspects of you as an individual. One may be to remind you of your physical structure and another to bring attention to your breathing or to your thoughts.

Look at your hands

Take a look at your hands. Now really look at them. Examine their shape, the nails, the skin folds at the knuckles, the protruding veins.

● Turn them over and examine the fine lines of your palm, the shape and size of it. Put your palms together and feel the sensation of skin against skin, the warmth or coolness of it.

● Let your fingers interlock, move those of one hand over the other to feel the texture of your skin, the sensitivity or roughness of it. Do the fingertips feel different from the skin further down your hand? Think about what function they have and all the different tasks for which you use them.

Put your feet on the ground

Take off your shoes (or keep them on if you would prefer that), and place your feet on the ground. If your feet are bare, feel the sensation of your feet against the carpet or floor. If your shoes are on, what do your feet feel like being in a restricted space?

● Bring your attention to the soles of your feet, the soft skin touching the surface below. Focus on the point of contact between the skin and the surface and start to be aware of this being a point of stability, of the ground being sturdy and strong.

● If you're feeling stressed or uneasy, sit at your desk, in a chair at home or even at a restaurant. Bring your attention to the soles of your feet touching the ground beneath you. Breathe naturally but allow your attention to be on the soles of your feet and how stable the ground beneath feels. Let this grounded feeling move up through your body.

Listen inside and out

Wherever you are, bring your attention to your hearing.

● Listen to the sounds that are close to you. Can you identify them? Are they gentle or intrusive, distracting or familiar?

● Extend the sound circle wider and listen to the sounds further away.

● Bring your attention back to those closer to you, gradually moving to the sounds within your ears. Do they ring, is there silence?

● Go within your body and listen out for the sounds of life within you.

● Listen to your breathing as you breathe in and as you breathe out.

An anatomy lesson

We all know how to breathe because if we didn't we would need external help. The fact that we know how to do something doesn't automatically mean that we know exactly what we are doing or whether we are doing it well.

We have a tendency to breathe into the part of our lungs that has the least amount of flexibility and space. The figures overleaf show the shape of the lungs within the rib cage and the umbrella-shaped diaphragm underneath.

You'll notice how the ribs towards the bottom of the rib cage aren't directly attached to the sternum or breast bone (the central bone running down the front of the rib cage). These are floating ribs as their ends are attached to the rib cage with cartilage which allows them to expand. Those directly attached to the sternum can't move in this way.

You'll also notice the shape of the lungs. They are narrow at the top and large at the bottom. Underneath the lungs is the umbrella-shaped muscle called the diaphragm. This muscle is attached to other muscles around the ribs and they work in a systematic way so that when the lungs need to fill with air, the rib space opens up, mostly around the area where the flexible ribs are situated, and the diaphragm drops down.

As you need to breathe out or exhale, the diaphragm begins to move up with the help of the muscles around the ribs, which contract, and this forces the air out of the lungs so they deflate.

This process is rhythmic and smooth and it takes place without us being conscious of it. It is an automatic process that is set at constant and it is this that allows us to breathe when we are awake or asleep, standing or lying, talking or listening.

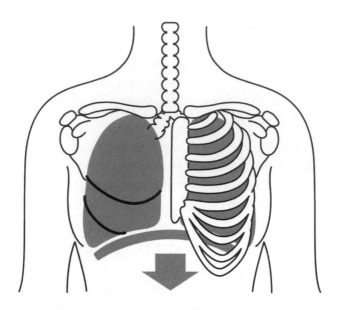

In breath – lower ribs move out, diaphragm drops down and lungs expand

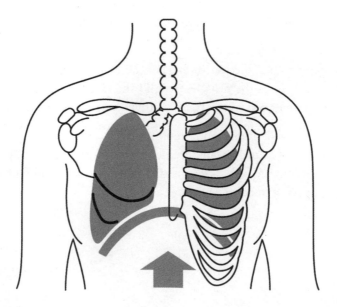

Out breath – lower ribs contract, diaphragm moves up and lungs deflate

The point of the anatomy lesson

- Take a deep breath. Hold it.
- What has happened to your shoulders?
- Remember to breathe out.

We often breathe in quite a shallow way, using the top part of our lungs more than the lower and larger part. This happens particularly when we are unfit, anxious, stressed or tense.

Mindful breathing helps train us to develop our physical breathing style so that we use more of the lower parts of the lungs. This type of breathing is often referred to as abdominal breathing and it is regarded as more relaxing and beneficial than shallow breathing. It's nothing new as you've been doing it all your life when you're more relaxed or asleep.

brilliant suggestion

- Breathe normally, without forcing it in any way otherwise you may feel dizzy.
- Place your hand on your chest and feel which parts of it move.
- Place your hand on your stomach and feel the movement.
- Notice the difference?

Place your hands on the sides of your rib cage (or someone else's if they're willing) and feel them in motion – how the ribs expand and contract when your breathing is shallow and when it is fuller.

On the move

What follows will be an unusual way of participating in an activity that is commonplace for most people. The aim is to use walking as an example of approaching an ordinary activity in a different manner.

You will need to go through the four stages a couple of times in order to become familiar with the concepts.

When walking we often focus on getting from one point to another and seldom do we take the time to experience the sensation of it – the feel of the ground beneath our feet, the slow and rhythmic movement of the ankle and foot as it steps down and is raised up, the air against our skin.

1 To start, take a walk in the garden, in the park or anywhere that is convenient. Keep your eyes half closed and let the focus be on your internal experiences and sensations, and that of your body and mind. Keep the objects that surround you, such as other people or the trees, at a distance in your mind.

2 Having done that, lift your eyes and bring into your awareness all the objects and movements around you. Allow yourself to be open to all of these and how they impact on you. Attend to the detail of each object and how it is placed within that particular setting.

3 Now move the emphasis on to the place that you are holding within this environment and the impact that you are having on it. Let the cycle of your breathing become balanced and be an integral part of this mini world around you. Notice your sensations, reactions and responses as you do this, and if they are different from how you normally would be within such a situation.

4 Finally, step back from such an active involvement and let there be a space between yourself and your immediate surroundings. Be aware of them and sensitive to them, but not fully a part of them. Again notice the difference in your sensations, feelings and thoughts.

A different sort of experience

You've been introduced to the idea of being mindful and how stress can affect you at so many levels. You've also read about and tried some of the everyday tasks that have made you aware of how little attention we sometimes pay to the small things in our lives that actually make up a large part of them.

- It would be useful to recognise whether or not you have actually tried any of the practices up to this point.
- If so, what has your response been?
- Did you scan over them, attempt a couple, notice anything different?
- If you haven't tried anything, how come?

The next practice is something very different from what you've done so far or may have experienced in your life. It is an activity that doesn't require you to be at all physically active but rather one that asks you to be alert and engaged with what is happening within your physical body.

It is good for lowering stress, helping you to feel less aroused or restless. Many people find it an excellent step towards better sleep, pain management and agitation.

Interestingly, men find this practice particularly useful and easy to engage with, perhaps due to its unobtrusive and practical participation. The practice is called Body Focus and that is what you'll be doing: moving through the different parts of your body and paying attention to them in a very different way.

We tend to focus on what is portrayed as an ideal shape and on how perfectly our bodies should function, forgetting that our bodies are as vulnerable and varied as are our minds and emotions.

▶ brilliant insight

We can develop distorted views of ourselves or imbalanced beliefs about our bodies when we suffer from stress, illness, chronic pain, depression, anxiety, trauma, addictions and weight issues.

The emphasis in this section is on your physical presence, and this is done through the use of the section on the CD entitled Body Focus (Track 1). A transcript of the audio material will be given in the event that you do not have access to, or are unable to use, an audio system of some kind. It is strongly recommended that you actually *listen* to each of the suggested audio pieces mentioned in the book as that is where the real work begins to take place.

> **IMPORTANT INFORMATION**
>
> All the practices are gentle, unintrusive and keep you focused on reality. You are in total control every step of the way. There is no suggestion whatsoever of you being moved into a trance or altered state of any kind. In essence, the emphasis is on helping you to be fully aware of yourself at this given moment. The following instructions will help you to prepare for the practice and settle into it.

Body focus practice

Time and place

Finding a time and place to carry out the practice is the greatest challenge. Turn off your mobile, ask others not to interrupt unless it's an emergency and recognise that this time is solely for you.

You *can* create a reasonably quiet place and space around yourself if you are willing to set limits and establish some boundaries.

Positions

Lying flat

It is preferable to lie on your back on the floor or the carpet, or lie on a mat or blanket. You can also lie on a bed or any flat surface if getting down onto the floor is difficult.

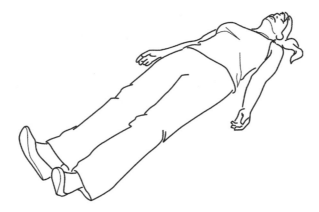

Legs can be straight or bent when lying on the floor.

You can lie down and place your legs on a chair, either straight or bent if that is easier on your back.

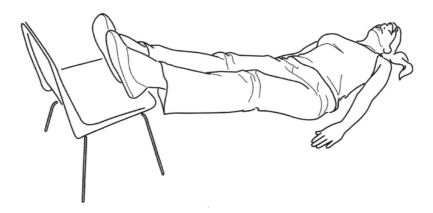

Use any supports necessary, such as a neck cushion, pillow or stool, ensuring that there is no unnecessary strain on your body.

Sitting in a chair

If lying down is uncomfortable or difficult, then sit in a chair. When sitting, it is important to check that the chair is high enough so that your knees are not higher than your hips. The chair should provide sufficient support, but again use footstools or cushions if necessary. Try not to be slumped in the chair.

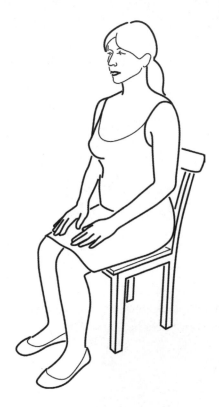

Standing

If neither lying nor sitting is comfortable then lean against a wall or stand, but take care that you have a firm object against which to steady yourself.

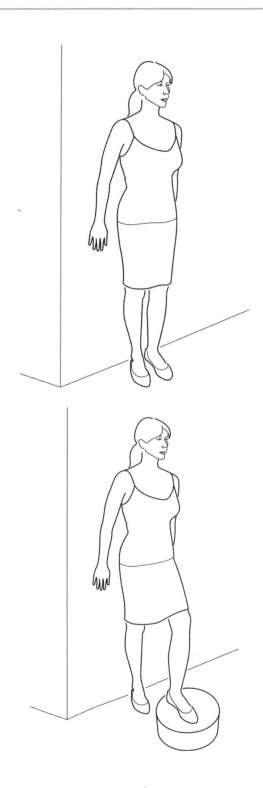

Clothing

Keeping warm
Wear sufficient clothes or cover yourself with a blanket as your body temperature will cool.

Be aware that when the instruction says 'Breathe into your hip' or any other part of your body the reality is that you can't physically breathe into any part of your body other than your lungs. It's about imagining the breath moving into that joint or section of your body and creating that image in your mind.

Reading the following practice and listening to it on the CD will be completely different. It really is worth listening to it and experiencing the sensations that come with it. Suspend judgement and you will be rewarded.

Body Focus practice (written version of Track 1 on the CD)

This is a body focus practice. To prepare for this practice, ensure that your clothing is loose and comfortable and that you have a blanket with which you can cover yourself.

Lying flat on the floor or on a bed is the favoured position, with your arms resting by your sides, palms facing upwards, or your hands placed on your abdomen. If you are unable to lie flat then bend your knees keeping your feet on the floor, or place your feet on a chair in front of you, being careful not to put strain on your back. Use whatever supports are needed to ensure that you are comfortable and taking care of your body.

If you cannot lie down then sit on a chair, letting your hands rest in your lap. If necessary you can stand but ensure that you have something to lean on for support should you need it.

Whilst doing this practice, the aim is to stay awake and alert, rather than drift off into a state of sleep. If you find over time that you are unable to stay awake then accept in a kindly manner that this is what happens and try changing your position or the time that you do this work.

Let us now focus on your body in a mindful and aware manner, taking care that you do only what you can and what you want.

Whether lying, sitting or standing, bring your attention to the point of contact that your body is making with the floor or chair. Notice which parts of your body are making contact – your head, back, your buttocks, legs and feet.

Allow your body to sink into the surface on which you are lying or sitting, feeling the weight of your body against it. Letting yourself be supported by the strength of the ground, trusting that it can hold you.

Bring your attention to your breathing, to your breath coming in and going out, to the rise and fall of your chest and with each outbreath allow your body to gradually ease, losing your resistance.

Feel the rhythm of your breathing, the ebb and flow of it as your body begins to respond: taking in with each inbreath and letting go with each outbreath. Allowing yourself to sink deeper into the floor or chair as your body begins to soften.

If you feel that you are going to drift off into a state of sleep, bring your focus back to the sensation of your breathing, keeping it as natural as possible.

The intention is to bring awareness to the different parts of the body without moving or stretching them in any way. It is about experiencing the sensations within your body, making no demands on it.

As you breathe in and out, become aware that this is your body, all of it, for whatever it is: the parts that work well and keep you alive, and the parts that are damaged and in pain.

Now focus on the big toe of your left foot. Become aware of the existence of this part of your body and the sensations that might be there. Let your attention go deep into the toe, not moving it, just observing it and feeling whatever is or isn't happening in it at this moment. If you feel no sensations that too is fine. Simply acknowledge whatever is there.

Now move your focus to the little toe on the left foot and to all the toes. Become aware of the feelings within the toes, acknowledge them, and breathe deep into the toes on an inbreath. And on an outbreath let go of your awareness of the toes, letting their existence drift and dissolve from your mind.

Now bring your attention to the sole of your left foot, focusing on any sensations deep within the foot, aware of the air against it, your instep, the heel against the floor. Breathing in and out of it and on the outbreath let go of your awareness of it and bring it to the top of the left foot, becoming familiar with the sensations in this part of your body, of all the small bones that make up the foot. Breathing all the way down into it, and then on an outbreath letting it dissolve from awareness.

Moving your focus to the left ankle, feeling and acknowledging whatever it is that is there, aware of the bones that come together to form a joint. Breathing into it and out of it, letting it go. Now focus on the foot and ankle as a whole, breathing deep into it. Let your breath travel in your mind's eye, all the way down from the nostrils, through the chest and abdomen, down the left leg and into the foot and ankle, aware of all the oxygen coming to it and when it gets there release and let the breath travel all the way back and out through the nostrils and on an outbreath let the foot and ankle dissolve from your awareness.

Coming to the left calf, what sensations are there at the top of the shin bone and deep underneath in the muscles that allow you to walk and move? Feel the sensations of all of the calf, the bones, the muscles, the skin that holds it all together, acknowledging these sensations while breathing in and out of the calf, releasing all tension from it. And on an outbreath, allowing your focus to drift from it and move to the knee.

Becoming aware of this area, of any pain or tension here. Breathing deeply into this part of your body, and letting go of it on the outbreath, and shifting your attention to the thigh. Feeling the largeness of the thigh, the powerful muscles within it, the sensation of it resting against the floor or chair, the shape and depth of it, all of it from the knee to the hip on the outside, and to the inner thigh by the groin as you breathe deep into it and out of it, and on an outbreath letting go of all your awareness of it.

And now on an inbreath, imagine the breath travelling all the way down the left leg from the hip and groin, down the thigh, into the knee and calf, into the foot and to the toes. And on the outbreath letting the air travel upwards from the toes, moving it all the way up eventually reaching the hip, and then letting go of any tension within it, and of your awareness of this leg.

Moving now to the toes on your right foot and the sensations within them. Breathing into them and out of them, then letting go of them. Shifting to the sole of the foot and the heel and moving around to the top of the foot, acknowledging what is there whilst breathing in and out and into the ankle. Now breathing deep into the foot and ankle as a whole, letting the breath reach all the way into this area and then letting awareness of it dissolve on the outbreath.

Focusing your attention on the right calf, its connection to the ankle and the knee, with its muscles and tendons. Aware of any sensations or discomfort, breathing in and out of it and now no longer giving it attention but moving your attention up to the knee, this part that often feels stiff or painful. Breathing into it, and letting go of it on the outbreath.

Attending now to the thigh, to the length of it, its depth and structure, its connection at the knee and hip, breathing into it and letting go of it on the outbreath and now letting your mind's eye take your breath down throughout the entire length of your right leg, all the way to the tips of your toes, and then all the way back up. And on an outbreath, let go of any tension in this leg and your awareness of it.

Aware now of the pelvis, the genital area, and all its sensations. Acknowledging any discomfort or tension. And now let your awareness include the buttocks and the contact that they have with the floor or chair. Recognising how this area is like a cradle, and allowing it to soften and to sink deeper into the floor with each outbreath and how each inbreath may bring with it new sensations. Breathing into this cradle and on an outbreath, dissolving awareness of it as you shift your attention to your lower back, to the spine with its gentle curve, to each vertebra being connected to the next as you feel them against the floor or chair, more aware with each outbreath as they sink a little lower into the surface. Becoming familiar with the sensations, sometimes of pain, sometimes of release.

And then gradually moving your attention into the abdomen, acknowledging the vital organs within this area, one by one. Aware of the life that these organs provide, each with its special function. Is there any tension or does this area feel soft and supported? Breathing awareness into all of this area, the spine at the back, the organs inside, and the abdomen and stomach as a whole, all held together … and letting the image of this area fade on an outbreath.

And concentrating on the spine further up, as the vertebrae and back of the ribs touch the surface that you are leaning against, aware of the shoulder blades, of any tightness or pain deep within, of the releasing and relaxing with each outbreath. Feeling the movement of the ribs as they expand and contract with the flow of your breath entering and leaving your lungs, whether it be fast or slow, easy or difficult. Aware of the sensations as you breathe, as the air moves down your throat, into the lungs and out again.

Noticing now the sound of your heart within your breast, the sensations where it is placed, its rhythm as it beats, pumping and renewing. Giving you life, beat after beat. Now letting the breath move all the way down the chest and into the abdomen, and on an outbreath letting go of all tension within this large area. Breathing deep into it, allowing it to soften and ease, and on an outbreath fading the image from your awareness.

On an inbreath, letting your attention move down into the hands of both your arms. Are the joints painful or stiff? Acknowledging this but also the loving and soft sensations when fingers touch or hands are held. Moving to the wrists and how flexible they are and then noticing the elbows as you breathe in and out. Feeling the sensations of the sensitive skin at the back of the upper arms and into the armpits … and then moving up to the shoulder joint where your arms attach to your trunk, and how it feels. Linger on these limbs, acknowledging their practical use and their ability to hold and to cradle. And on an inbreath, breathe all the way down from the top of the arms to the tips of the fingers and on an outbreath, let the breath travel out, and awareness of this area dissolve.

Bringing the focus to the tops of the shoulders, to the area that so often is tight. What are the sensations here, is there tension, are the shoulders resting unevenly? Not moving any part, but simply knowing and becoming familiar with what is happening in this part of your body. Now breathing into and out of this area and to the back of the neck and the skull, allowing the tension to soften with each outbreath, releasing any tightness in the throat and letting your neck sink gently into the shoulders and towards the floor.

Paying attention to the jaw. Are you clenching it or is it open and relaxed? Becoming aware of the softness of the mouth, the sensitive sensations within this area, the tongue within this space, the air touching the back of the mouth and throat. Notice how the tender skin at the back moves as you breathe in and out, allowing the air to move into the lungs. And on an outbreath, letting go of this area from your awareness.

And moving your attention to the nostrils and the air caressing the skin as it enters and exits. The sinuses that often throb, the sensations around the eyes, the tension that spreads into the temples on the sides of your head and the ears, perhaps your hair touching them, or deep inside a ringing sound. Aware of all the sensations in the different parts of your head as you breathe in and out. Not forcing the breath in any way, but allowing it to move naturally as you attune yourself to your body, and then on an outbreath, letting this part of your body fade from your attention.

And as you lie here or sit, become mindful of the sensations of your skin, that vast span of protection that is a container for each and every part of your body. Your whole existence, physical and emotional, carried within this breathing and flexible container but often only acknowledged when it is damaged or wrinkled. Give your attention to it and the sensations of it as the air or clothing touch it as you slowly float your awareness of it from the tip of your head, moving gently all the way down the length of your body, front and back, to the soles of your feet and when you have reached the soles of your feet drift your attention all the way back up over the skin to the top of your head.

And now, imagine you have a hole at the top of your head and into it is coming the breath and vitality of life. Allow it to enter and flow through each and every part of your body, into the bones, muscles, organs ... moving into the smallest and deepest parts of your existence as it travels down, flowing smoothly and gently, nourishing and feeding everything as it moves towards the tips of your toes and letting it out through your toes, renewing itself and coming back into your body, travelling all the way up with its energy and purity, leaving through the hole at the top of your head. And without forcing it in any way, let your body sink into the ebb and flow of this vitality as it glides into your body at your head ... drifts out through the toes, and rolls up again, bringing with it a state of deep relaxation and stillness. Opening to a calm and tranquil feeling of healing, of completeness.

Gently gather your breathing and awareness back into your skin, back into your lungs, and into your body as a whole. Awaken all your senses, knowing that you are one unit, breathing and functioning in a state of completeness, bringing with it a kindness and compassion for yourself, for your body, for your existence. Focusing your attention on this moment, being present here, right now, in this place, knowing that your body and your presence are firmly but gently supported by the space around you,

and the anchoring of your breath within you, centring you, balancing you,
giving you the strength to be alert and alive in each moment of your life,
for whatever it brings.

Once you have finished the practice you may want to go through the
questions below.

Questions to ask yourself

- Did you make the time and privacy to do the work suggested?
- What was it like doing it?
    - could you concentrate on the task?
    - what sensations and discomforts did you feel in your body?
    - were there any feelings of anxiety or pleasure?
- Did your body parts feel connected or disjointed as you went
  through the practice?

What happens to your body when you are distressed by physical or emotional difficulties?

- Where in your body do you feel it?
- What do you feel in your body at that time?
- Where is that feeling right now?
- Has the physical pain led to an emotional response (e.g. irritation,
  depression etc.)?
- Have your emotions triggered a physical reaction (such as
  stomach ache, difficulty in breathing, a headache) or a craving for
  a drug/alcohol/food?
- What thoughts come into your mind at times like this?

Making links

There has been discussion on how the mind and body are interconnected and how our bodies can respond to our emotional or
psychological state. As a follow-on to the discussions, it would be

helpful for you to think about the links between what is happening to you, or what you are feeling, with how you react to it.

The following questions are a place to start.

> Mindful breathing is about bringing your focus to breathing in and breathing out

- How do you cope with physical pain or discomfort?

- What do you do when you're feeling emotionally distressed or upset, even angry or agitated?

- Is there any link between your physical state, your feelings and your thoughts? For example, if you have a headache and need to rest but your partner wants to talk to you, do you become irritable which leads to your shouting at your partner, which in turn leaves you feeling guilty and ashamed?

- What do you do when you feel this way?

- Does whatever action you tend to take work for you? For example, does taking a pill, going for a walk, withdrawing, having a drink, shouting at someone or going on the internet achieve what you want it to?

- Do you wish you could deal with certain things in a different way?

brilliant suggestion

- Each day, stop for a few moments, close your eyes and listen.
- Open your eyes and look.
- Integrate the sights and sounds into your experience and awareness.
- Notice your thoughts and feelings.
- Be here, in this moment, for a moment.

brilliant example

James was a manager in a media company. He was involved in an accident that resulted in his bones healing but his being left with tremendous pain. He became increasingly distressed by the memories of the accident and the pain. He was agitated and frequently irritable, he felt depressed and often became withdrawn, he couldn't sleep even with medication and the use of alcohol. His family life had deteriorated, his work was being affected and he was traumatised by the events surrounding the accident and the accumulating consequences of it.

After an explosive and frightening outburst he eventually entered therapy where mindfulness work was introduced. The idea of his trying something like this was alien to him. On the one hand, therapy helped him with his difficult memories and depression, but being able to listen to the mindful practices at home in his own environment and have time to think about how to implement the concepts helped to turn his life around. It took work and a decision to keep at it that made the difference but what really hooked him in was the effect that the Body Focus practice had on him. He would listen to it on a regular basis as he felt it eased his pain and allowed him to keep connected to where his pain was at a particular point and how he responded to it.

As mentioned in the previous case studies, it was through the combination of considering the concepts of mindfulness and its approach to life and doing the practices that allowed change to come about. Not only did his pain become far more manageable but his use of powerful painkillers decreased dramatically. His angry outbursts at small issues dissipated and his family relationships didn't only return to normal but became closer and more satisfying.

It would be inaccurate to put the transformation down to mindfulness alone as he was working through his trauma in therapy at the same time. Perhaps the extent of benefits came about because he was able to work at different levels with his distress. He could discuss his intense emotions and reactions, be made aware of psychological understandings as well as mindfulness concepts and take these away with him. He could then use them in his everyday life and work with the practices so that it all became integrated in a real and ongoing way. He preferred using the Body Focus practice although he did use the mindful breathing 5-minute meditation on a daily basis.

This highlights the fact that you don't need to do everything at the same time and that you can choose what works best for you, knowing that you may want to experiment with new or different practices over time.

A note of caution: Mindfulness can work well with therapy and medication but it shouldn't be used on its own if there are overwhelming feelings of distress. If you need to talk to someone then that is what you must do. Mindfulness is powerful and strong feelings can come to the fore, so it is best not to do the practices on your own without support if there is underlying trauma, mental health conditions or serious addictions. In addition, you should never stop your medication or treatment without discussing it with your healthcare professional nor should you suddenly stop drinking or using drugs if you have been using them in higher quantities or to excess.

> Mindfulness is not a therapy nor is it a substitute for talking therapy or medication

This chapter has looked at how our minds and bodies are interconnected and why abdominal breathing is important. The mindful practices included short and simple ones such as placing your feet on the ground as well as a more formal one of Body Focus. Occasionally, it feels like an effort to get going with a formal practice but you'll notice that it only takes a few minutes to feel engaged with it.

The following chapter will outline a series of body movements as a way of extending the mind–body connection concept. The idea is to encourage you to engage with these in a mindful way so that you'll be integrating body awareness and movement with breathing and mental focus. Remember that the practices are being outlined in detail as the assumption is that you are new to this. For this reason, care has been taken so that you can engage with the practice in a beneficial and safe manner.

 **brilliant** recap

- We are mind and body not mind or body.
- We work as one unit with each part affecting the other.
- Breathing is our life source so it makes sense using it to our best advantage.
- You've been introduced to some of the mindful practices.

Our bodies talk to us even if we aren't listening,

CHAPTER 4

Mindful movement

The integration of mind and body is an important component of mindfulness as it realigns our minds with our bodies and our bodies with our minds. The aim is to assimilate these two parts of ourselves and in this chapter it is through our bodies and our breathing.

A mountain in the wilderness

This short activity that follows, called The Mountain, may remind you, or help you to recognise for the first time, what it is like to feel a sense of stability and firmness in the world no matter how off balance you may be feeling at this point. By going through it on a regular basis it can help you to feel resilient and strong.

As with the Body Focus exercise, there will be a few suggestions on how to go about this practice as well as a written description of the audio material. Again, listening to the material and experiencing it is very different from reading it and its real effect can only be felt when you are engaged with it.

This posture focuses on creating balance and stability. It does not require any movement but rather concentration on the sensations within you. Breathe normally and gently at all times.

Instructions: It is essential that you take care with any practice by ensuring that you are in a safe place and that you don't attempt anything where you may put yourself at risk, such as standing on your own without support if you are prone to falling over or leaning against a chair that can slip.

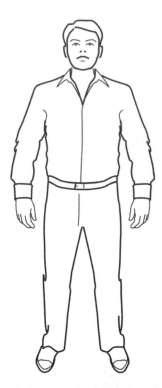

The Mountain (written version of Track 3 on the CD)

Stand with your feet hip width apart so that you can balance yourself. Keep your knees soft and your hips loose, imagining there is a small weight attached to your tailbone (coccyx). Tuck your navel in towards your spine as though you are pulling in your stomach to tighten your belt. Relax your shoulders into your back, lightly tuck in your chin, and let your head balance on top of your spine. Breathe in, and on an outbreath let unwanted tension be released. On an inbreath take in a feeling of relaxed strength.

As you stand, be aware of your breath moving in at the nostrils, down the back of the throat, into the chest and down into the abdomen, and then its movement from the abdomen, through the chest and throat, and out through the nose. Allow a natural rhythm of breathing; not forcing the breath in or out in any way.

While standing here, feel the weight of your body in your feet, firm against the earth and that the earth can carry your weight with confidence. Let your breath feel as if it is moving all the way down into your feet, giving them strength and stability. Now let the breath move into your ankles, strengthening them, and now into the calves. Let it flow into your knees, without locking them, and then into your thighs. Move the breath and steadiness into your hips, genitals, buttocks and abdomen, and let this area of your body feel strong but relaxed.

Allow the breath and strength to move up your spine at the back, through your stomach and chest, eventually reaching your shoulders, checking that they are relaxed. Your arms becoming stronger and part of the mountain, stabilising you, balancing you. Let it move into your neck and jaw, into the skull, ears, face, eyes and right up to the top of your head.

Now, in your mind's eye, move the breath to the base of your spine and thread it like a piece of string through each vertebra from the tailbone, up through the pelvis, the lower back, the middle of your back, the shoulder blade area, the back of the neck and all the way to the top of your head where it exits and is held gently but firmly on a hook, allowing your body to hold itself.

Feel the sensation of this, of your body standing like a mountain, fixed and firm, gracious and solid. The mountain is stable and grand: the earth beneath it, the sky and air around it. The weather changes, the seasons move from one to another but the mountain remains. Feeling the strength of the earth beneath you, solid and powerful, and your body open and alert, as you stand grounded and dignified in this space.

The Mountain practice may have reminded you of what it is like to stand still on your patch in the world. It doesn't matter where your feet are on the ground in terms of location (at work, home, in the park, outside a shop, on a hospital ward), they can always be firmly rooted to that spot for that moment. In that way, you can stand grounded and dignified in this space no matter where you are in the world.

brilliant suggestion

The Mountain practice is not specific to mindfulness as it is used in many other areas such as in drama classes and public speaking training and one can understand why. It is also a good practice to use with children, particularly with those who find it difficult to concentrate or stay still for any period of time. A few of the phrases

▶

and words can be changed to suit the age and ability of the child and it is also a nice thing for parents to do with their children as a joint activity. The other practices can also be used with children in the same way.

You have now experienced the Body Focus practice and the Mountain one so you're beginning to get a feel of what it is like to connect with your body in a different way. You've perhaps managed to do the walking practice (*On the move* section) where you could experience the sensation of slowing down even when moving and of playing with how you can engage or disengage yourself from your surroundings, being part of them or detached from them.

> Do these practices because you care about your life

The following section is an outline of simple body movements that can assist you in your everyday life. The most basic of movements have been chosen as it is all too easy to launch into some form of exercise without giving sufficient consideration to your current physical limitations.

Mindful body movements

The traditional movements associated with mindfulness programmes have been yoga based. Part of this tradition comes from the fact that various forms of yoga originated in the same areas of the world as the ancient practices of mindfulness. This tradition came across to the West when the mindfulness-based stress reduction programme (MBSR) was developed as practitioners based it on what they had learnt in Buddhist teaching centres.

Yoga is an excellent form of exercise as it focuses on body and breath. However, caution is essential as it can be quite hard on a body that is not particularly subtle or that is not used to such types of moves. A more integrated approach is favoured here wherein a combination of gentle yoga, Pilates and physiotherapy exercises is used.

For some, even these gentle moves are not possible as you may be severely ill, in a wheelchair, bedridden, in pain or too frail. Should this be the case, other exercises can be implemented. The point is that whatever one does, no matter how small, it can be done in a way that integrates the movement with your breathing in a mindful and caring way.

These movements are only suggestions and are not a substitute for continuing with any other intervention you have been recommended. Hopefully, they will ease you into gentle activity if you've tended to shy away from it in the past.

- It cannot be emphasised enough that you should only attempt what you can.
- If you have any physical difficulties then have someone nearby who can assist you if needed.
- Stand on a nonslip surface in bare feet or in nonslip shoes.
- Ladies – no heels and remove your jewellery.
- Gentlemen – no socks and remove your jackets.

brilliant suggestion

Why not do the moves with someone else? One person talks it through while the other does it and then switch around. That way both of you get to do it and can be of help to each other.

Standing movements

As with the Mountain, to begin, stand with your feet hip width apart so that you can balance yourself. Keep your knees soft and your hips loose, imagining there is a small weight attached to your tailbone. Tuck your navel in towards your spine as though you are pulling in your stomach to tighten your belt. Relax your shoulders into your back, lightly tuck in your chin, and let your head balance on top of your spine. Breathe in, and on an outbreath let unwanted tension be released. On an inbreath take in a feeling of relaxed strength. This is referred to as the neutral position.

Recall the balance and stability you felt when doing the Mountain practice and start the following exercises from that posture.

Be aware of each movement and let your breath flow in and out, without forcing it or breathing too deeply.

Shoulder shrugs

The first is the Shoulder Shrug. Standing in the neutral position, let your arms hang loosely by your sides. Breathe out, lift the shoulders up towards the ears. Hold them there, breathe in, and as you breathe out, relax the shoulders down into the back. Repeat 3 more times.

Shoulder circles forwards

The next move involves shoulder circles in a *forward* direction. From a neutral point, bring your right shoulder up to the ear, rotate it forward, down, around the back, and then towards the ear and continue with 3 more circles.

Move now to the left shoulder and repeat 4 times, returning to the neutral position.

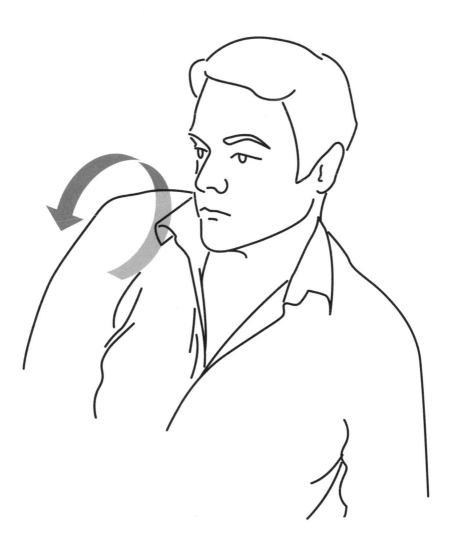

Shoulder circles backwards

We will now do *backward* shoulder circles. From the neutral position, lift your right shoulder up to your right ear, then rotate it back towards your shoulder blade, down towards the floor, forward and then up to the ear. Continue with 3 more circles, relaxing your shoulder at the end of it.

Move now to the left shoulder and repeat 4 times, returning to the neutral position at the end.

Chest stretch

Check your posture so that your feet are hip width apart, your shoulders relaxed and your head gently balanced. Let your arms be at your side. This move is like a bird spreading its wings out to the side and then bringing them in again. So, with your arms down cross your hands in front of you. From this position, inhale while you extend both arms to shoulder-height, arms parallel to the floor, and on an outbreath, bring the arms back down so that your hands cross over each other. Repeat this 3 more times in a flowing movement.

Now, doing the same movement with the arms, spread them out but as you are bringing them down to cross your hands, gently bend the knees at the same time, and as you lift the arms up again, straighten the knees. Repeat 3 more times at an easy pace then relax your knees and arms.

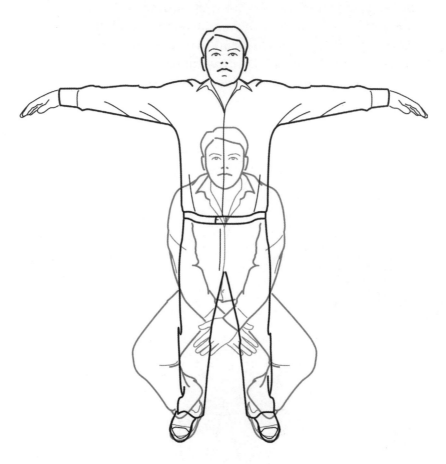

Neck and shoulder tension release

With soft knees, and relaxed but strong shoulders, gently tilt the head forward so that your chin moves towards the chest and then lift it to the neutral position. Don't tilt the head back. And again, slowly drop the chin and raise it, and gently drop it and raise it, and finally lower the chin and come back to the centre.

Now with relaxed but erect shoulders and soft knees, gently turn your head to the left, bring it back towards the centre and then turn it to the right in one flowing movement. Without forcing it repeat this 3 times and then bring your head back to the centre.

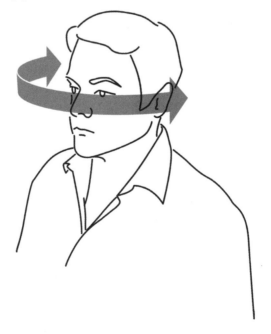

From the neutral position, gently tilt your left ear towards your left shoulder keeping the ear in line with the shoulder so that your head isn't tilting forwards. Keep your shoulders relaxed. Only go as far as is comfortable and breathe into it (count to 8). Come back to the centre. Now tilt your right ear towards your right shoulder, keeping a straight line and not forcing it (count to 8). Come back to the neutral position. Repeat and return to the centre.

Now breathe out and slowly drop your head to your chest releasing any tension, breathe in and as you breathe out raise your head back to the neutral position. Repeat 3 times.

Full arm circles

The following movement is a full arm circle. Be careful not to breathe too deeply but rather to allow the flow of breath to go with the movements.

Standing in your neutral position, bring your hands to cross in front of you. Breathe in as you start to circle the arms around with the arms crossing as though you are removing a jumper or T-shirt, continue with the circle breathing out as the arms come down (see overleaf). Breathe in and continue the circle upwards, breathe out as your arms come down. Repeat twice more then relax the arms by your sides.

Arm lifts

The focus will now be on lifting the arms (see opposite). Standing upright, breathe out and lift the right arm up in front of you all the way until the back of your hand is up towards the ceiling, keeping the elbow soft and the arm rounded. Breathe in and bring the arm down towards your side. Repeat this 3 more times. Relax the arm and move across to the left arm and do the same.

Arm lifts alternating

Both arms will now be used, but we will alternate them (see overleaf). Keeping the same posture as before, check that your hips are facing straight ahead and that your weight is evenly spread. Arms by your sides, lift your left arm towards the ceiling and as you bring it down the right arm lifts up towards the ceiling, so that they are crossing over with the one arm following the other.

Repeat this 3 more times but after the fourth keep both arms *raised* and with your arms above your head ...

Upward stretch

... lift your left arm towards the sky pointing your fingers upwards. Breathe into the stretch, keeping your feet flat on the ground and your shoulder relaxed. Reaching up straight.

Relax the left shoulder a little and switch to the right arm, stretching the fingers towards the sky; reaching up as though trying to pick a cloud out of the sky, without tilting or overstretching. And now relax the right shoulder and stretch again with the left one, breathing into the stretch, and relax that shoulder and stretch with the right arm, breathing into it. And on an outbreath bring both your arms down to your sides, becoming aware of the changes in sensation in your hands, arms and torso.

Side Bends

This next movement involves gently bending sidewards. Still in the standing position, shoulders relaxed into your back, hips facing forwards, feet apart and knees soft. With your arms relaxed down by your sides, breathe in and on an outbreath gently run your right arm down the side of your right thigh so that you are bending your body from the waist and allowing the left side of your body to be stretched. Only go as far as you can. Watch that your body is in a straight line and that you aren't leaning forward or twisting your shoulders. Breathe in, and on an outbreath come back to the standing position using the muscles in the core of your body to lift you and not your shoulder. Check your posture and repeat 3 more times, remembering to breathe and to bend from the waist in a straight line. Return to the centre.

Repeat 4 times on your left side, remembering to breathe, to return to the centre using your core muscles and to bend from the waist. Notice the areas of tension and when you tend to stop breathing. Return to the centre at the end.

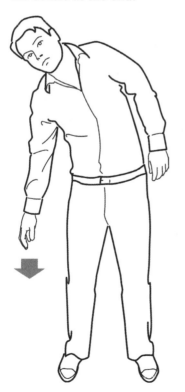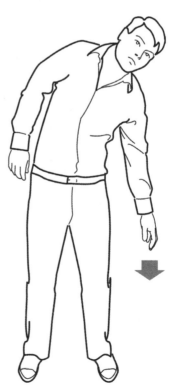

Floor movements

Now place yourself on the floor, if you can, as the following moves will be done lying on a mat or soft carpet.

Foot circles, foot flexes and one-leg circles

Lie on your back with your knees bent. Roll your hips slightly to ensure that they are evenly placed on the mat or carpet. Check that your spine is keeping its natural C-shaped curve in the small of the back. This is the relaxation position.

Bend the left leg towards the chest and clasp your hands *behind* the left knee, not *on* the knee but on the back of the thigh just below the knee, so that your calf is parallel to the floor. Gently circle the left foot clockwise 4 times, keeping the movement continuous.

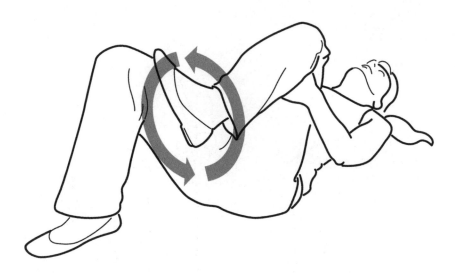

Now circle it anticlockwise 4 times.

Check that the upper part of your body is relaxed. Still holding your thigh, point the toes of the left foot towards your chin and then in the opposite direction away from you, repeating this 4 times, remembering to breathe naturally.

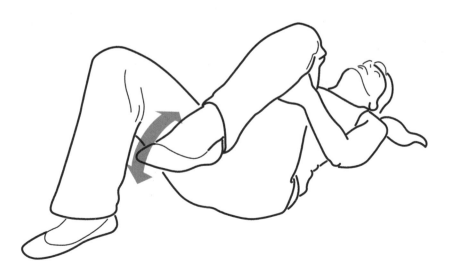

Now hug your left knee closer to your chest, releasing the tension.

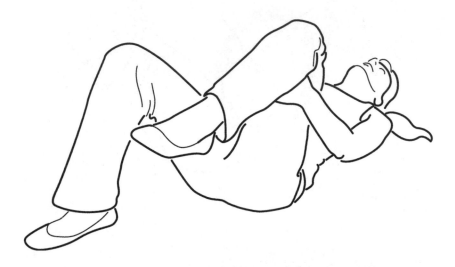

Release your hold on the leg and extend the same leg up towards the ceiling but keep the knee soft and have the leg about halfway up. You want to mobilise the hip joint so let the focus be there and not on the knee. Keep your hips still and relax your upper body. Now, circle the leg clockwise 4 times keeping the circles small (see opposite). Now do the same, but in the other direction. Lower the leg and return to the relaxation position, that is on your back, feet on the floor and your knees bent.

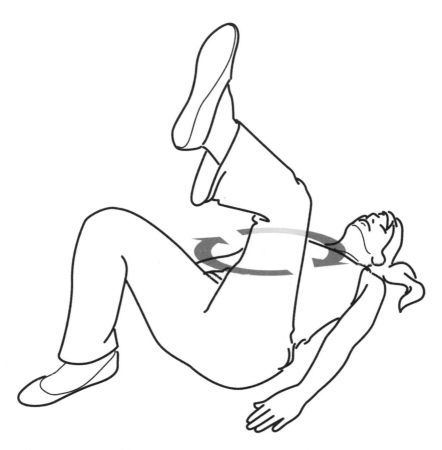

Check that your hips are evenly placed on the floor, and now bend the right leg towards the chest and clasp your hands *behind* the right knee on the back of the thigh, having your calf parallel to the floor. Repeat the sequence of foot circles clockwise and anticlockwise, toes pointing towards and away from your chin, knee hugs and hip mobilising circles. Remember to breathe. Lower the leg, and come back to the relaxation position.

Pelvic tilt

We will now get the pelvis and lower back moving. So, lying on the floor, knees bent, feet hip width apart, and the spine in its C-shaped curve, check that your hips are even and that you aren't putting more pressure on one side than on the other. Relax the upper body.

Breathe in, engage the pelvic floor muscles and pull your navel towards your spine. As you breathe out, start to press your waist into the floor so that your pelvic area begins to rise, slightly curling the pelvis inwards.

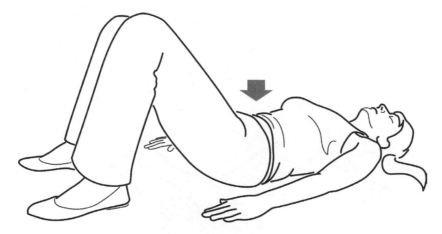

Keep your hips on the floor. Hold it there, breathe in, breathe out, breathe in, and on the outbreath slowly roll the pelvis back to its neutral position. Repeat the sequence 3 more times.

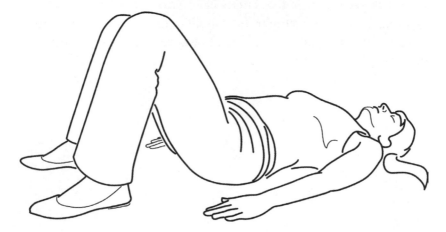

Windmill arms

The focus will now shift to the arms. In the relaxation position, so still on your back with your knees bent, have your arms down by your sides, elbows soft and open. Breathe in, breathe out, taking navel to spine. On an outbreath, lift the left arm above the head going back towards the floor behind your head. Keep your shoulders relaxed and watch that your spine isn't arched. Breathe in and bring the arm down to your side. Now repeat the move 3 more times.

Now move to your right arm and repeat 4 times.

Now alternate the arms (see opposite). So, keeping the spine length-ened by releasing the shoulders into the back raise the left arm towards the floor behind you and when you are returning it to your side, raise the right arm behind you so that as one arm goes back the other comes forward, crossing in the middle. Repeat this sequence 3 more times. Place the hands down by your sides, and be aware of your breathing and the sensations in the upper part of your body.

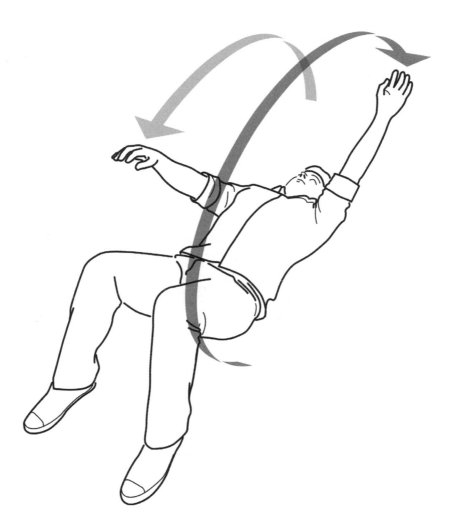

Shoulder bridge

This next movement is a little more demanding, as you will be lifting the hips up towards the ceiling. Only do what you can and stop if it hurts. Lying on your back in the relaxation position, breathe in, engage the pelvic floor muscles and navel to spine.

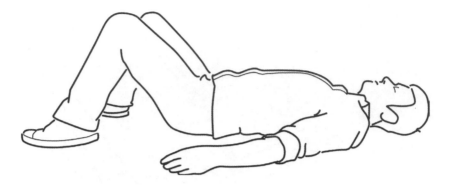

Breathe out and start tilting the pelvis towards the ribcage. Gradually peel each vertebra off the floor, one by one, lifting the hips up. Take each vertebra off the floor, going as far as the shoulders but not all the way to the neck. Let the strength come from the abdomen and buttocks so that you don't put pressure on your neck. This takes you to a position where your abdomen and thighs are like a ramp or bridge. Once there breathe in, out, in and as you breathe out, starting at the neck imprint each vertebra back into the ground, one by one, so that you return to your relaxation position (count to 6). Now repeat it, breathing out, peel each vertebra off the floor, from the tailbone, keeping your pelvis and abdomen strong, lifting the hips but without putting pressure on your neck. When you are at shoulder height, breathe in, out, in and then as you breathe out roll each vertebra down starting at the neck imprinting it onto the floor until you are back in your relaxation position. Repeat twice more.

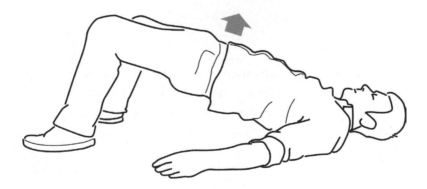

Finishing off

Roll onto your side. Carefully and gradually bring yourself up from the floor, pausing for a moment before standing up. There is no rush and be cautious not to force or jar your body.

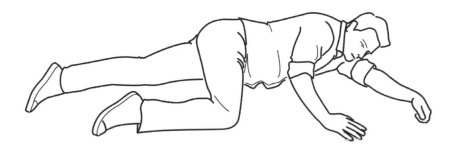

✴brilliant suggestion

Try getting the feel of one or two movements and become familiar with them before moving on to the next one or two.

This will help you to know which ones are manageable and which are too painful or difficult.

We don't need to be attending the gym or running around a field in order to keep fit. The gentle moves provided in this chapter can help to introduce you to more body fitness or to restart it. They can also be used in conjunction with other exercises or even adapted to suit your situation. Whatever the case, taking care when exercising and breathing correctly when doing so is important for our health and safety.

The next step of the mindfulness work is for you to be introduced to mindful breathing in a more formal way. This practice will highlight how difficult it is for us to keep our minds focused. However, using this practice will help you in remarkable ways as well as train your brain to make new connections and reinforce others.

brilliant recap

- It's usually because we don't have the interest or desire to learn new things rather than that we're too old to do so.

- Keeping mobile and subtle is essential for our health.

- We can do this in a variety of ways.

- Remind yourself that you can stand dignified and grounded wherever you are in the world.

We forget how much emotional tension we hold in our bodies.

CHAPTER 5

Keep breathing:
steadying
monkey mind

This chapter will introduce you to the final practice in the book which specifically focuses on mindful breathing without the use of body movements. It will provide you with a shorter and longer version of the practice so that you can find which length of meditation suits you. In addition, attitudes and assumptions are questioned regarding your view of life as well as how much of your life you live outside of the present moment. The breathing meditations help to train you to focus on the immediacy of this moment and to bring your attention back to it. It is through the *continual* use of mindful breathing that you will be able to refocus your attention, increase your concentration and help your brain to engage so that it can respond in a positive, resilient and helpful way.

Ruminations and assumptions

Life is a series of breathing in and breathing out. It is a continuum of events, both known and unknown, and not a cycle as we cannot move back or around, only forward. We can move and be with the change or frantically build brick walls in a futile attempt to protect ourselves from the universal motion of change.

We use up so much energy reliving the past and creating a future. We go backwards and forwards, in and out, up and down but what we seem to find most difficult is to be here: to be still, to be in the moment, to be completely present in our own lives at this moment.

We assume that there should be no difficulties or hardships in life, that suffering is an unexpected setback and that struggles mean life is out of balance. The reality is that that is life and mixed in with those things are times of happiness, joy, abundance and all that pleases us. Life is not happy or sad, good or bad, easy or hard, it is all of these things in different measures at different times but always together.

The same goes for us as people. We aren't all good or all problematic, we aren't perfect or failures, we are a combination of all these and they too co-exist within us and show themselves depending on the circumstances and situations of that time. The trick is being able to allow such contradictions and fluctuations to be part of us and our lives without them being destructive through actions, self-criticism or judgement.

We sometimes expect from ourselves or our lives what we would never expect from others or the universe. Seasons may bring less or more light and warmth but not one at the complete exclusion of the other. We are the same. At certain times we feel more in control of our lives and the situations that surround us and at other times we feel as if our worlds have gone into a state of chaos. When we look more closely at those disruptive or harsh times we can see, sometimes only in retrospect, that there were a few things that still held our lives together and perhaps even gave us pleasure or joy.

Being mindful can help us to tolerate the difficult times without necessarily feeling overwhelmed by them and allow us to see some of those brighter flickers of light even when it all may appear dark. It won't remove the pain or let the laughter last forever but what it can do is help us keep balance when we feel off balance.

Focused awareness

Mindfulness can also be referred to as focused awareness or intentional awareness. The key element is about bringing your attention and focus to the present moment with intent. Intent implies that you have an objective in mind, a purpose or aim and that is to be engaged with whatever is happening in this very moment of your life. Aware of what is happening within you, noticing it, observing it and being with it. You can then make a choice about what you would like to do or how you would prefer to respond rather than react impulsively or unthinkingly to what it is that is happening.

There is an emphasis on both your internal responses, such as disappointment or fear, and your external responses such as an angry outburst or refusing to speak. Becoming aware of your internal responses can help you to monitor your external or behavioural responses. An example of this would be instead of having a few drinks and cigarettes, reaching for a pill, watching porn, placing a bet or pushing past someone on the train you can recognise that you're tense and go for a walk or talk to a friend. You could do some mindful breathing, listen to music or simply refocus your attention onto something that eases the tension.

▶ brilliant insight

It is difficult to do something about a situation or state if you don't know what it is. Once you can notice and acknowledge it then you can take a decision on what to do next.

Awareness isn't something that comes easily to us. For some reason, it is seen as having no purpose and being limited in value. It is often associated with those who are therapy junkies, navel gazers or slightly neurotic and needy. This dismissive attitude towards self-awareness encourages the spread of hurt, disruption and destructive patterns of behaviour. People may engage in harmful and hurtful behaviour towards themselves and others, damage their health through poor self-care, excess or a devil-may-care attitude towards their drinking, raised blood pressure or stress levels. They may realise they are harsh, selfish or unkind in close relationships but do nothing about it even when their partners have left or their children have distanced themselves. A manager may be controlling and unsupportive towards staff because he or she feels inadequate but may prefer to make their lives unbearable and let them leave rather than attempt to be different.

Mindful breathing

The following practice can't easily be explained on a page. Its intrinsic value and benefit can only be felt and encountered at a more fundamental level when it is experienced. The remarkable thing is that it is nothing more than focusing your attention on your breathing. To state this makes it seem as if there is some catch, some strange and hypnotic process that will be woven in at a secret and subconscious level. Be assured, there is no such process. Just as you focus your attention on an object of interest or concern, so you would bring your attention to your breathing and focus on it. It may sound easy but you'll probably change your mind once you've tried it.

There is a catch – the more you do it the more you will benefit from it but you need to actually do it and keep doing it.

We all have 5 minutes

It is probably best to start off with a 5-minute meditation (or mindful breathing practice if the word meditation is off-putting). Remember, it's about breathing with intention and focus, a little like getting yourself to take a deep breath when you're feeling tense. In this instance, it is more than one or two breaths and it is both to decrease stress or distress as well as to help prevent it.

Don't be afraid to try it. After all, you're already breathing.

brilliant suggestion

- breathe as naturally as possible without forcing the breath in any way
- if you breathe too deeply you may feel dizzy
- keep in mind what was said about abdominal breathing and breathing into the largest parts of the lungs rather than the more restricted shoulder area
- keep at it, even if only for a couple of minutes at a time, as you'll soon wonder how you ever did without it

Positions for mindful breathing practice

It is best to be seated for these practices as it allows you to sit in a tall and dignified position.

Chair

If you're in a chair, then place your feet on the ground and have your back slightly away from the back of the chair. Hands can be placed on your knees or in your lap.

Floor

If seated on the floor, cross your legs, ensure your knees are not too far above your hips and that you are sitting in an upright position. Hands can be on your knees or in your lap. Be careful not to slouch or to have your chin jutting out. Sit on a cushion or stool.

You can lie on the floor with props if that is most comfortable though it is sometimes more difficult to stay awake in this position.

Lying on the floor with your knees up or on a chair is also a possibility. This can be used by those who find it difficult to sit upright, are in pain or are weak. Use any props that may add to your comfort.

Bed

If you're unable to sit in a chair then sit up in bed or lie down. The important thing is that you are able to stay awake.

Standing

If you are only able to do this in a standing position then it would be wise to ensure that you can lean against a wall or firm surface, that you are sufficiently awake so that you don't feel drowsy and fall over and that you move your position if you feel off-balance. You can raise one leg onto a stool as that can help to take strain off your back.

Remember:

● stay awake
● use any necessary props and keep warm

- you can be in any position – it doesn't matter
- never do these practices at a time when you should be concentrating on something else such as driving, working machinery, walking along the road
- do it at a time when you're more alert rather than in bed after a long day
- if you're uncomfortable, move but do it in a gentle way and think about what you're doing
- your mind will frequently drift and your concentration lag – that's fine – keep going
- this is not a competition – do what you can, when you can, as long as you do it

Mindful Breathing practice (5 minute version of Track 5 on the CD)

With your eyes closed, being alert and awake, bring your attention to your breathing and to the movement of the breath as it comes in and out of your body. Simply observe your breathing – watching the path it takes as it travels in at the nose, down to the abdomen and then out again through the nose.

Staying focused on the breath without forcing it in any way. Being here, with each inbreath and with each outbreath, letting one follow on from the other.

Use your breath as an anchor. Allow the breath to anchor you to the centre within your abdomen, that part that is stable, focused and present. Follow the breath to your anchor, bringing with it a new beginning and with each outbreath a letting go.

Be aware of each breath nourishing and grounding you, renewing and letting go, one breath following the other. Allow it to bring with it a stillness and a feeling of balance, grounding you right here, right now. Letting it anchor you, gently and kindly, to this moment ... and to this moment.

As the intensity begins to ease, let your attention spread to include all of your body and engage your breath in a rhythmic flow that moves in and out of your body as a whole.

Gradually let your awareness begin to take in the sounds around you and within you, simply letting them exist in harmony with you as you breathe. Sitting in stillness, in this moment. Feeling grounded, feeling balanced.

Gently allow all of your senses to be awake, to be alert and alive to all that is happening within you and around you. Acknowledge with kindness that you spent this time living each moment of your life, with whatever came with it, in a mindful, balanced and open way and that you now have the choice of how you wish to live this moment of your life ... and this moment.

Now that you've read the transcript, if you haven't already, listen to the CD.

Monkey mind

You'll have noticed that there are no peculiar instructions and that the words are simple and familiar. Give some thought as to how you felt doing this short practice. Probably the first thing that you'll say is that you found it hard concentrating. The good news is that everyone finds it difficult, the bad news is that that is what happens and you'll find your mind drifting even after years of doing it. We all do because that is what our minds do – they drift and float, they wander off in many directions no matter how determined we are to keep them fixed in one place. It is best to get used to this process as there is no getting away from it. The more you train yourself to bring your mind back to your breathing the easier it will become and the longer you'll be able to focus. Longer may mean twenty seconds today but tomorrow may mean five seconds or five minutes. That's the way it is.

This ability to focus is part of jumping off the hamster wheel. We all have *monkey minds*, as the Buddhists call it, which is a wonderful description of how our minds tend to jump here, there and everywhere with squeaks and squawks. They throw things at us, grab other things and generally have more energy and activity than that of a hyperactive two-year-old having a tantrum.

Taming the tantrum

There are no tantrums but simply a mind that can either be left to run amok or one that can be settled and helped to ease our lives. It's about managing our minds and how we work with ourselves and what comes up in our heads and our hearts.

> Our thoughts are only thoughts, they are not facts. We don't need to attach ourselves to them

The longer version of the Mindful Breathing practice (also referred to as Mindful Awareness or Mindful Meditation) that follows will give you more instructions on how to help manage your thoughts. We tend to believe that we are our thoughts, that they define us. They don't – no matter how kind, harsh, embarrassing or shameful they are. Thoughts are only thoughts and they can come and go just as anything else can. Our lives are filled with things that change shape, move and evaporate. The same applies to our thoughts as they aren't fixed structures. We may believe that they are immovable but when we observe that they can come and go then we can start to recognise that we don't need to become attached to them in the same way as before.

Mindful Awareness (20 minute version of Track 7 on the CD)

To begin the practice of mindful awareness, find a time and place where you won't be interrupted and give yourself this time without pressure or criticism, and accept the care and nourishment in a gentle and compassionate manner. Mindful awareness is about becoming aware of what is happening within yourself, for whatever it is, and using your breath as an anchor in order to accept and manage it.

Try and remain alert and awake throughout, knowing that there is no judgement or expectation.

With your eyes closed, being alert and awake, bring your attention to your breathing and to the movement of the breath as it comes in and out of your body. Simply observe your breathing – watching the path it takes as it travels in at the nose, down the abdomen and then out again through the nose.

What sensations come with your breathing?

Staying focused on the breath, without forcing it in any way. Being here, with each inbreath and with each outbreath, letting one follow on from the other.

Gently check your posture for any tension in your body and, in a kindly manner, carefully bring yourself back to the position of openness and alertness while continuing to focus on your breathing.

If your mind has drifted off into thoughts or ideas acknowledge this without criticism and gently accompany it back to your breathing, to each inbreath and to each outbreath. Your mind will wander, as minds tend to drift and float. Without judgement, gently escort your mind back to your breathing no matter how many times this happens. Allowing yourself to be present, in this moment, for whatever is happening.

Use your breath as an anchor. Allow the breath to anchor you to the centre within your abdomen, that part that is stable, focused and present. Follow the breath to your anchor, bringing with it a new beginning and with each outbreath a letting go.

Be aware of each breath nourishing and grounding you, renewing and letting go, one breath following the other. Allow it to bring with it a stillness and a feeling of balance, grounding you right here, right now. Letting it anchor you, gently and kindly, to this moment ... and to this moment.

Should you feel discomfort in your body, either mindfully shift your posture or breathe deep into the discomfort. Allow your breath to soften the area, let it open and ease, staying with the sensations and any changes that may be happening.

As the intensity begins to ease, let your attention spread to include all of your body, and engage your breath in a rhythmic flow that moves in and out of your body as a whole.

Now become aware of the sensations within your body that involve that of touch – the buttocks making contact with the cushion, your feet touching the ground, your back against the chair, whilst you breathe into the whole of your body.

Allow yourself to be aware of whatever it is that you are feeling, wherever it is. Staying right here, in this moment, fully aware of your breath, your sensations, your body being here, open, dignified and complete.

Bringing your attention back to the breath if your mind has drifted off into yesterday or tomorrow. Simply being here. Anchored, balanced, alert.

Gradually let your awareness begin to take in the sounds around you and within you, simply letting them exist in harmony with you as you breathe. Sitting in stillness, in this moment.

As you sit here, let your awareness move to your thoughts. Just observing them from a distance, not attaching to them. Letting them be there while you watch them come and go. Simply let them come to the fore and let them pass on. Using your breath as your anchor, finding the balance within your mind and your body of being grounded and aware, but not attaching yourself to your thoughts.

Allowing the flow of your breathing to keep you present, within this moment, while you sit here.

Feeling grounded, feeling balanced. Gently allow all of your senses to be awake, to be alert and alive to all that is happening within you and around you.

Acknowledge with kindness that you spent this time living each moment of your life, with whatever came with it, in a mindful, balanced and open way, and that you now have the choice of how you wish to live this moment of your life ... and this moment.

brilliant suggestion

When you're feeling stressed, distressed, in pain or are craving, place your feet firmly on the ground, if appropriate, and put your hand on your abdomen. Breathe in and out, aware of your hand moving up and down. Focus on the rhythm and movement of your breathing and you'll soon begin to feel more settled.

You may be wondering if it is worth all the effort of making time, working at the practices and trying out suggestions. If you've come this far then it is likely that you're still interested. You've been made aware of a range of different practices that you can use as well as discussions around life issues. The next chapter will take a look at your attitude towards yourself and how you treat yourself as this too is an aspect of mindfulness and one that can help encourage and motivate you to give more thought to your life.

brilliant recap

- Breathing is fundamental to being alive.

- Mindful breathing helps you to train your brain.

- It assists with reducing stress, managing your monkey mind and lowering your levels of arousal.

- You may only focus for a few seconds at a time or a few minutes and that is fine.

- Don't give up even if you're thinking about six different things. There is still benefit gained by doing it.

- The more you do it the greater the benefits.

Our feelings are far more powerful than our thoughts.

CHAPTER 6

Taking care of yourself

Being mindful and bringing mindfulness into our lives is also about bringing kindness and care into it. We cannot begin to shift our approach to life and ourselves with mindfulness if we ignore how harsh and judgemental we are about what we look like, how we behave and what we feel. We are sometimes nothing short of brutal towards ourselves when we make a mistake, fail an exam, aren't successful in an interview, a relationship falters or we are struggling. If we translated our thoughts into physical actions we would realise how abusive we can be and the extent to which we batter ourselves. We then wonder why we feel downtrodden, depressed, anxious, angry or defeated.

As with awareness or insight, compassion and kindness is all too often relegated to the tree-hugging brigade. When we are kind to ourselves and not critical of the action, pain, feeling or thought it can then be seen for what it is and recognised as being part of ourselves rather than something we want to disown.

We need to question whether being harsh and critical actually motivates us or hinders us. In the past, there was a view held by some that the more you pushed yourself with critical feedback

> Taking care of yourself is an act of kindness

the better you would do. It was a culture of *no pain, no gain*. However, when it comes to our emotional and psychological health this tends to work against us rather than assist us. When we show kindness and consideration to ourselves we are more inclined to feel less depressed, stressed and anxious. This type of self-care and understanding builds

resilience and well being and it can create a more balanced and positive view of ourselves and our lives.

How do you react to yourself?

- If you make a mistake what do you say to yourself?
- If you're on a low-fat diet and you eat a packet of crisps what happens?
- How do you respond if you fail an exam?
- What do you do if you play badly in a match with a partner and lose?
- How do you feel if you shouted at your partner for no apparent reason?

What words or phrases do you use when you're being self-critical?

Do you have a favourite one?

Does all this judgement and cruel language make a difference or do you feel twice as bad about what happened? The answer is probably that none of this really helps you to feel any better about the situation or yourself. Think about the look of despair and distress on a child's face when scolded by a parent in a harsh and angry voice. That is what you do to yourself. Just as with the child, it doesn't matter what outward response is shown, you will walk away feeling despondent, humiliated and ashamed. The effect of that on an ongoing basis is neither helpful nor healthy.

You are still responsible

Being considerate and kind to yourself and showing some compassion and understanding is not about shifting responsibility or dismissing what you do. It is about cultivating an environment in which you can notice and alter what works for you and shift what interferes with the good. If you plant a seedling, you need to give it food and water and have it in the right place in order for it to grow into a healthy and strong bush that can withstand the different weather conditions. If you withhold water and insist on stamping on the ground around the delicate roots because it isn't growing fast enough then it is likely that the bush will grow in a distorted shape and only partly thrive, if at all. We are no different as people. We have an innate drive to survive but the conditions in which we grow and develop will affect us throughout our lives.

Self-care and kindness is not about avoidance or denial. You are the one who is being hurtful, destructive, angry and sabotaging to yourself and maybe to others too. These are your behaviours and reactions so the responsibility lies firmly in your court, but being harsh and abusive to yourself won't give you the motivation to do something constructive about them. Care, kindness and openness will.

Neither is it about self-pity (*poor me, life is horrid only to me*), or inflated self-esteem (*I'm better than you so I feel good about me and I am entitled to have whatever I want*). It is about self-compassion, which gives you the message that you deserve understanding and tolerance. This is very different from making excuses for your actions.

Mindfulness is not therapy

Mindfulness can help us recognise some of these patterns and anxieties and, in turn, allow us to soften our approach so that we can start dealing with them. It should be restated that mindfulness is not therapy and it shouldn't be used as a substitute for it. It can help bring about a level of understanding and insight, which in itself can stir up difficult feelings, but what it can't do is help us to gain the depth of understanding and make the links between what has happened in our lives and how we have reacted to those experiences. Going into therapy and talking about what has affected you is about taking responsibility. It is a caring and important decision that shows that you can take yourself seriously and that you respect your life.

There is so often a fear that therapy will dredge up awful and terrifying things and that you'll only get to know of the difficult or horrible aspects of yourself. This is far from the truth of it. People are surprised at how little they have acknowledged their strengths and goodness. They begin to recognise how much criticism they inflict on themselves and how they have taken on beliefs about themselves that are damaging and cruel and yet untrue. Therapy is there to help address issues at the same time as build your resilience and sense of worth. It may feel like a bumpy ride at times, but it needs to be otherwise the distressing stuff that drives you to be destructive or harmful to yourself will remain covered. It is when it is understood with kindness and placed within the context of your life that you can make sense of it and begin to make shifts.

Make friends with yourself

When we meet someone new we ask them questions about themselves and take an interest in them if we like them. If we get to trust and love them, we become more open and accepting of them, we see them as friends and trustees of our emotions and thoughts, we are grateful for their being in our lives and we make an effort to protect and care for them. We take risks with them, we reveal our bits of quirkiness and our vulnerabilities. We love them and hate them, often at the same time. We hold them when they are upset, laugh with them when they trip over in life and forgive them when they anger or embarrass us.

We need to do the same with ourselves.

brilliant suggestion

- Sit quietly, take a few breaths and repeat the following to yourself:
  - may I be happy and healthy
  - may I be free from pain and suffering
  - may I accept myself for all that I am
- Repeat these phrases a number of times no matter how difficult it feels and even if you believe you don't deserve the goodness of them.

You can change the wording to what suits you but it must be within the spirit of allowing yourself to have something that is good, kind and generous. This practice is referred to as a loving-kindness or compassion practice.

Just as you are responsible for your actions so you are responsible for your health and emotional wellbeing. Taking care of yourself in an open and generous way is of primary importance as it allows you to take on new ideas, rethink old ones and generate ways of interacting with yourself that increase your capacity to enhance your life. Remember, we all have 5 minutes in a day to give ourselves.

Caring about your life includes recognising when it is off balance and finding a way to manage the situation, as well as yourself, so that you can reset the point of balance. The following chapter will look at different concerns and provide suggestions on how to help shift them.

brilliant recap

- Being respectful and caring towards ourselves is an act of kindness.
- Judgement and criticism stifle us, they don't motivate us.
- Taking responsibility for yourself and your life reminds you of the times when you do have choice.

Life catches up with us.

CHAPTER 7

Managing difficult times

ife isn't only about harsh and distressing times and we shouldn't focus on those alone. Throughout the book you have been encouraged to develop a greater sense of mindfulness so that you can enjoy the good times as well as find the resources to deal with the difficult ones.

A framework for mindfulness follows as a summary of the points mentioned in previous chapters. It is a structure upon which you can build and create a mindful life for yourself. Following this, a selection of difficult issues has been chosen, each containing thoughts on it in addition to a useful suggestion that may help you deal with the situation.

A mindset

Mindfulness is about bringing heart into your life and it encourages you to focus attention on the various facets of yourself. It allows you to like even the most difficult parts and to build the resilience and strength to manage life, even when it feels unmanageable. It is a mindset that weaves its way into all aspects of your existence, particularly when you use the more formal practices, as it brings it alive and provides you with the moment-to-moment experience of what to do when you need to or want to. You literally train your brain and your psychological structures to respond. The science of it is there and is clearly seen on scans. Remembering this can be very helpful as it can reinforce your use of these concepts and practices as well as modulate your scepticism or reluctance.

It would be repetitive to go through the key aspects of mindfulness with each of the situations mentioned below so it may be best to lay out a basic framework from which you can work and refer to whether you are reading about managing your life, your health or your depression. The sections on these aspects will include a few tips and comments to assist you, though what is said in one may well apply to all the others.

Mindfulness framework

- Mindfulness is an approach, a mindset, a way of being.
- It is accompanied by practices that are key to shifting your life.
- It centres around being alert and aware, awake and responsive, to what is happening within and around you within this moment.
- It encourages an *approach* rather than an *avoid* mindset, a turning towards rather than a turning away.
- Pay attention to your life and to what happens inside you.
- Slow things down, which will allow you to recognise more of what is happening.
- Allow whatever you are feeling and stay with it for whatever it is.
- Be aware of your interactions with yourself and with others.
- Notice, observe and acknowledge your reactions and responses.
- Get to know whether you're reacting or responding.
- Be curious about yourself and interested in yourself.
- Give your emotions space to exist, whether it be fear, joy, anger, stress, distress, pleasure, pain, depression, hurt, addiction, disgust.
- Breathe – it is the source of life.
- Be kind, caring, gentle and open to yourself.
- The more you use mindfulness the more resilience and resourcefulness you'll develop.
- It gives you a sense of control over your responses and how you manage your life.
- It provides a space between your thoughts and your actions, your feelings and your expression of them, your desires and your options.

- It provides you with choice.
- Use the practices because they work – the more you do them the more they help.
- If you don't try it you'll never know if it can be of help.

Stress

We live in a stressful world that demands our time and in which there is extensive information competing for our attention. We are on call 24 hours a day, seven days a week. Think back twenty years to how comparatively little information was thrust at us compared with now. Life is transportable. Accessibility and convenience have increased, but the other side of this is that we are flooded with demands, phone calls, emails, advertising, noise and many other things. It is no surprise that we feel tired and stressed out so much of the time.

There are also demands and expectations that are part of life, such as meeting the needs of children, having a job, working on a project, caring for a partner or relative, helping a friend, keeping ourselves fed, clothed and in a decent living space and so forth.

We need to take stock both of our expectations of ourselves and of those others have placed on us, which we try to live up to. It doesn't matter if it is at work or at home, within ourselves or from others. It is our responsibility to sift through what is appropriate and what is inappropriate and to set limits. Frequently, it is we who place excessive demands on ourselves through our perfectionistic ideals, our exacting expectations, our fear of failure or criticism, our difficulty in saying no and in asserting our opinion. If the stress is from an external source, such as a boss or partner, then it is helpful for you to discuss your concerns with them and for you to set boundaries. If you cannot do

> Life is stressful. It is up to us to set limits so that we take care of ourselves

this, then it comes back to you recognising that part of it is your difficulty and that you would benefit from understanding why you struggle to assert yourself.

At times we know that we are taking on too much and pushing ourselves too hard but we don't want to change the situation because it serves a purpose. For example, caring for a sick relative fills a gap of loneliness for us or taking on too much at work helps us to avoid problems at home or in a relationship.

brilliant suggestion

- Acknowledge to yourself that you are stressed.
- Denying your stress and distress won't make it go away. It is your responsibility to do something about it.
- Keep perspective. Ask yourself 'Is it worth getting stressed over?' 'Is it worth ruining my health over this?' 'How serious is this?'
- In your mind, step aside from the stress so that you're outside the circle that is creating it. See it for what it is and be mindful of how you are reacting.
- If it's serious, deal with the crisis then deal with yourself.
- Take responsibility. Remind yourself that you have a choice about how you're going to deal with this moment.
- Focus on breathing in a mindful way as in the exercise below.

Breathing exercise

- Bring your attention to your breathing.
- Breathe normally without forcing it in any way.
- Count silently or out loud if you want.
- On the inbreath count 1, 2, 3, 4 or say 'in', 2, 3, 4.
- On the outbreath count 1, 2, 3, 4 or say 'out' 2, 3, 4.
- Continue with this until you have settled.

Anxiety and depression

Feeling anxious or depressed may be due to stress, concern about what others think of us, thinking poorly of ourselves, fearing criticism or failure, or because we don't believe we are good enough, pretty enough or something enough. It may be a consequence of past experiences and the impact they have had on us, or the beliefs we live out from what was instilled in us by parents or significant others. Anxiety may be more in the area of our thoughts or manifest itself in heart palpitations, sweaty palms, shortness of breath, shallow breathing, tense jaw, tight shoulders or a knot in your stomach.

Depression may take the form of feeling lethargic, a loss of interest, withdrawal, loneliness, flat mood, poor sleep, overeating or poor eating, poor concentration, difficulty in carrying out tasks as well as you did them before, a feeling of sadness, being tearful and generally not wanting to engage with people or life as you once did.

It can show itself as agitation or aggression. Men, more so than women, become agitated when depressed as they tend to find it difficult to express their deeply-felt sadness and feelings. They may be less familiar with identifying their feelings and with the words used to articulate emotional states.

The medicalisation of depression as being a chemical imbalance has prevented people from realising that their feelings of depression are in response to events, experiences or circumstances that have happened in their lives. These may be a series of different incidents or one major event from the past or present, or from both. It is frequently about layers of experiences that affect how we feel and those in turn then impact on the next layer.

Taking a pill for anxiety or depression may flatten the distress but it is unlikely to remove the cause of it. This is not suggesting that you stop your medication but rather highlighting that we often turn to pills, alcohol, drugs, sex, food or risk-taking to ease our distress rather than actually address the underlying factors. It is only when you deal with those ideas, drives, feelings and beliefs that there is any real possibility of the positive effects being achieved and maintained.

If you rely on alcohol or pills, for example, then take those away and you go back to the same position as you were in at the beginning and sometimes it is even worse. This is where your taking responsibility for yourself and your wellbeing comes into play. You are the one who can make the choice. Think of it this way: if there is a crack in the road and you cover it over with a thin layer of tarmac it will be functional for a time, but there is a likely chance that the crack will reappear and perhaps be deeper and wider than before thereby increasing the risk of damage.

brilliant suggestion

- It is sometimes wise to reconsider your concerns.
- Place them in imaginary piles – those that belong to you, those that were placed on you by significant others and those that are a result of the expectations of the culture and society in which you live.

Anger

Anger can be the flip side of depression. If the sadness, pain and hurt cannot be expressed in one form it will find another way out and sometimes it does this through anger as it is a more readily acceptable outlet (not abusive, violent anger but a more everyday type of anger).

Anger for some seems easier or less embarrassing to show. Regardless of whether it is about depression or not, anger is a powerful emotion and we aren't always taught how to manage it without it being damaging or hurtful. It can eat away at us and its potential for explosion is an unpleasant feeling for the individual as well as frightening for those around him or her. We use terms such as 'lash out' or 'explode' when we talk about anger and we usually see it depicted in drawings as someone 'steaming' with it. This intensity of feeling, whether it is shown or not, is neither physically nor psychologically healthy.

brilliant suggestion

- Denying your anger won't help to deal with it.
- Accept that you're angry.

- Step back from it and count to 10, stamp your feet, jump up and down or walk out of the room.
- Focus on your breathing or use the breathing exercise suggested in the Stress section.
- When you are more settled, think about why you felt so angry and what you can do about that specific situation.
- Think more about what you need to do about your anger in general, if it is a wider problem.

Sleep

Sleep is essential as it is a time when the body can be restored and rested, when our minds can process the information of the day and when we can have some time out from ourselves. However, many people complain of insomnia or interrupted sleep, which can affect our health, psychological functioning and mood.

Sleep difficulties may be due to a variety of reasons. Our minds may be too active as we haven't given ourselves sufficient time after a stimulating situation to wind down, we may be worried or angry, ruminating on events or feelings, we may be stressed, anxious, depressed or agitated. There are other reasons too, such as noise levels, too much alcohol, being too full after a meal, a sick child, a restless partner, pain and so forth.

Falling asleep or remaining asleep can also involve us having to trust that we can take time to rest without full awareness. If we are anxious or untrusting of our worlds then we may find it difficult to let go and believe that we will be sufficiently protected through the night.

brilliant suggestion

- If your mind is on the go and you can't fall asleep ask yourself if you can do anything about it at this hour of night and at this exact moment.

▶

- If you can't, then step aside from the thoughts, feelings and ruminations and focus on your breathing.
- Pay attention to each inbreath and each outbreath.
- You can count 1, 2, 3, 4 as you breathe in and 1, 2, 3, 4 as you breathe out.
- Remind yourself that sleep is the time for your mind and body to recuperate.

Difficult or traumatic memories

Traumatic or highly stressful situations can be very disruptive to our state of mind, affecting us at a number of different levels including memories that intrude into our minds, loss of interest in things we once enjoyed, poor sleep, difficulty concentrating, hopelessness, anxiety and depression, being over-alert and feeling that our lives have been altered in some way.

Difficult situations do not always lead to traumatic memories, but when they have been sufficiently disruptive and have affected us for a period of time then we need to consider their impact. They may have been a long series of experiences of a physical, emotional, sexual or verbal nature or one major incident such as assault, a road traffic accident, a heart attack, a sudden illness that requires emergency intervention, a near-death experience, an unexpected dismissal from work, a partner walking out unexpectedly or the sudden death of a loved one. Common and key features are that the experience affects us on an ongoing basis, it intrudes into our minds with or without reminders of it and it leaves us with a high level of arousal or anxiety.

It is helpful to find ways of lessening this arousal and working with the memories so that the intensity of their impact can be calmed and decreased. Mindfulness can help lower your arousal, anxiety and depression but it won't directly deal with the memories and their impact on your life.

As previously mentioned, the breathing practices can help to lessen your protective defences and thereby allow the memories to push through in a powerful way. For this reason, it is important to have a support system already in place when doing the practices if the trauma or memories feel overwhelming.

brilliant suggestion

It may be worth talking to a professional healthcare person about this as such experiences seldom fade into the background and often influence our lives in obvious, or less obvious, ways. Speaking with someone is just that. It doesn't mean that you aren't coping or are weak but it does provide the opportunity for you to talk about what has happened and your reaction to it. If your car is involved in an accident you'll take it to the garage for repairs so that it can continue to function in the best way. You wouldn't continue driving it with a leaking water pump and a broken headlight. The same should apply to us as people.

Weight management

If we had to separate what we eat in order to survive and what we eat because of our moods, lifestyles and desires then we would probably notice that there are two very distinct piles of food. We eat, overeat, under-eat or eat poorly for different reasons. We may have little interest in our health or dislike cooking so we eat convenience food; we may be feeling lonely, depressed, scared, angry or bored so we use food to stuff down our feelings. We may use food to nurture ourselves or we use being overweight as a way of keeping people at a distance in order to avoid intimacy.

Food is central to our survival but it is closely aligned to our family dynamics, upbringings and cultural and societal attitudes. Aside from this, what we tend to forget is to pay attention to exactly what we are eating, how it tastes and how we eat it. Taking more notice of this, slowing it down and recognising it can have an impact on your eating patterns and can help you to manage what you eat and its quantities.

- Eat a meal alone without people, TV, music or reading to distract you.

- Let your attention be on the eating of that meal.

- Be aware of each mouthful, its taste and texture, how often you chew before swallowing and whether you put more food in your mouth before you've swallowed the previous portion.

- Note what it is like and how it differs from other meal times.

Pain and illness

Pain, whether acute or chronic, hurts and it affects our lives at many levels. Our quality of life decreases if we are ill and/or have pain. We find it harder to socialise, engage with activities, be with others, keep focused, sleep, breathe, eat, perform at work or sexually, men may become impotent, women may lose interest in sex and our moods fluctuate. Around 50 per cent of people with chronic illness become clinically depressed but this often goes undiagnosed. Life can change quite dramatically depending on the severity of the pain and/or illness.

We tend to lose belief in our bodies and this impacts on our state of mind. We no longer think that our bodies can support us and provide us with the mobility or internal activity that is needed to get us through the day and night without worry.

People with chronic and severe pain often find that medication cannot provide complete relief. Medication may reduce the severity of the pain or even stop the progression of the illness or disease but seldom does it allow for ongoing absence of pain. Emotional states of mind can exacerbate levels of pain and even be a factor in the development or continuation of a condition. This isn't to say that an unexplained condition is simply in your head or that your mood creates your arthritis, cancer or back pain. What it suggests, as previously mentioned, is that we work as mind and body, as one unit that is interconnected so one will influence the other. Once we are aware of this, we can begin to recognise how we often experience more pain when our mood is low or when we are upset or tired than when we have heard good news or are engaged in a pleasant activity. By the same token, if we are constantly distressed by the level of pain we are experiencing it is difficult to feel cheerful and well.

brilliant suggestion

- When in pain, remind yourself that the pain is a part of you, not all of you.
- It may not feel like it at the time, but there are parts of you that don't suffer from pain.
- Breathe into the pain - it can help to lessen the intensity of it.

Loss and grief

Death is what usually comes to mind when one talks of grief or loss but it can be there for other reasons too. It could be through divorce or separation, the loss of a job or status, a miscarriage, loss of functioning through illness or disease, a change in life circumstances, rejection, abuse, loss of what one had through an accident or illness, assault, rape, domestic violence, sexual abuse and so forth. In some instances, there is a sense of loss for what we never had and the opportunity for it has now passed. We are told it will be all right but sometimes it doesn't feel like it will and we are overtaken by the intensity of the pain and suffering. We are seldom listened to without being given advice, nor are we taught how to work with our distress and manage it.

The idea that we should be strong and get on with life may have some merit but, in real terms, it does more to deny our pain, sorrow and fear than motivate us to keep going. Avoiding, pretending and skirting around our feelings will only force them to come out in some other form such as overeating, health problems, withdrawing, being aggressive, drinking, smoking, gambling or being agitated or depressed. Sometimes we put protective barriers around ourselves in an attempt to prevent further sadness or despair, which is understandable, but that can inhibit us from being involved with new relationships that could possibly bring with them some love and care.

brilliant suggestion

- Remind yourself that even though you are feeling overwhelmed by the distress and sense of loss there are some aspects of your life that you are managing, no matter how small.
- When the emotional pains grips you, let it be and breathe into it.
- Once it has eased (as it will), tell yourself that what you feel today is not necessarily what you'll feel tomorrow.

Fear

Another pervasive and underlying factor is fear. Fear often propels us to do things that we know aren't necessarily in our best interests, may stretch our moral and ethical beliefs or work against our health, happiness and wellbeing. When we are driven by fear we become stressed, anxious, distant, overprotective, defensive, isolated, angry, alienated, physically ill, aggressive and cut-off from pleasure.

brilliant suggestion

- Let there be space for your fear.
- Let it exist and be cared for rather than avoided.
- Don't give it the power to control your life.
- We are all scared of something.

Shyness

Shyness goes hand in hand with fear and anxiety. Being shy is not necessarily a problem but if it interferes in our lives so that we are timid, inhibited and withdrawn to the point where we prefer not to go out or engage with people or activities then it can be a problem. Our quality of life can be affected as we may refuse going on dates, having sex, travelling, playing sport, taking a better job or attending a party as a way of protecting ourselves from our fears and concerns. This can lead to us becoming restricted in our lives which in turn can result in us feeling lonely and isolated and having less in our lives than we perhaps could have. It may result in us becoming depressed or using other means, such as alcohol, to boost us or relying on internet interactions and pornography to meet our needs in place of face-to-face interactions.

brilliant suggestion

- Keep in mind that others too are self-conscious but that they may not show it.
- Remember, if you scratch the surface of anyone's life you'll get to hear of their fears, anxieties and self-consciousness.
- Tell yourself that you have a place in the world – your own patch that belongs to you no matter where you are or how small it feels.

Shame

This is one of the unrecognised toxins within us that permeates through to our beliefs about our worth. Shame is a response to our self. It can come about as a consequence of an action or powerful thought we have had or else from what we have come to believe about ourself from what another person has said to us. Examples may include cheating in an exam, stealing, being cruel or abusive, lying, being deceitful or hurtful. Shame differs from guilt in this context. Guilt reflects more on the action of what we did and we think we shouldn't have carried out that action. Shame reflects on our opinion and view of ourself, our image of our standing in our own eyes.

Shame can be instilled in us by others. Parents may be harsh or unkind to their children, telling them they are unlovable, ugly, stupid, useless or the like. This can also come from significant others in one's life or even from a boss. We feel a profound sense of embarrassment about a fundamental aspect of ourselves at a deep level, such as being unlovable as a person, unworthy of being cared for or ashamed about our bodies. This may have been accompanied by having felt humiliated by what another had said or done and then that became part of the shame one feels.

Shame can have a strong influence on us as we can carry it with us throughout our lives. It can affect our relationships, our levels of intimacy and our interactions. We feel we need to keep ourselves protected so that others don't get to see our shame or shameful parts. It can create isolation, fear and loneliness as we can become withdrawn and separate ourselves from others. As with shyness, we may use unhelpful means to alleviate our distress or to give us the chemical bravado to mix with people. It can affect our work, our careers and our social interactions as we either constantly doubt our abilities and therefore sabotage our promotions and relationships or else we over-compensate for how we feel and become bullying, over-controlling and dismissive of others' needs.

brilliant suggestion

- Ask yourself what you're ashamed of or feel shame about.
- Where it comes from (your action or someone else's).
- Do you need to cling onto it so hard?
- Is there any room for you to reconsider this feeling or belief?
- What if you no longer felt like this, what would you do and could you manage it?

Addictions: substance misuse/gambling/internet use/pornography

Food, drugs (prescription, over the counter and illicit drugs), alcohol, gambling, exercise, social media outlets and pornography are some of the activities and substances to which we can become addicted. As with the term *trauma*, we need to be careful not to dismiss our actions or regard them as being acceptable simply because they do not fit into a predetermined category or meet the criteria for a formal diagnosis. On the other hand, it isn't wise to misconstrue behaviour and see it as a true addiction when it isn't. Perhaps one way to judge for yourself is to, firstly, be honest with yourself about the extent of it and secondly, to recognise the real extent and impact that these behaviours have on your life.

If your relationships, level of functioning or work is being affected then there is a problem. If you think it helpful to have a couple of shots of alcohol before you go out in order to boost yourself and then need more when out socialising in order to really enjoy yourself then there is a problem. If you enjoy pornography more than the realness of a sexual relationship with others then there is a problem.

In other words, it is relative. Using something external doesn't imply that you are addicted to it, but when it is more satisfying, gratifying and enjoyable than life without it and you can't honestly do without it then it may be helpful to think about how much impact it is having on your life and whether or not you should be recognising that there is an imbalance.

An over-dependence on anything is generally a sign that all is not what it should be. When you feel agitated that you can't have access to, for example, the internet, pornography or a gym for a period of time or you prefer yourself if you've had a few pills or drinks and think you'll have a nicer time with them and not such a good time without them then you may be dependent on them. Not necessarily addicted but dependent or over-dependent. When this moves up the scale then addiction begins to set in.

It isn't always the extent of use that should determine whether or not there is a problem but how it affects your life at a personal and inter-personal level.

Try this experiment:

Do not attempt it if you know that you are highly dependent on alcohol or drugs as you could go into withdrawal and become unwell.

- Refrain from the action for a week (having a drink, cigarette, drug, chocolate, exercise class, pornographic film, smart phone, internet use, gambling bet or anything on which you usually rely).
- Could you do it?
- If not, how did you respond?
- Did your mood change, were you agitated, anxious or irritable?
- Were you craving and, if so, what did you do in response to it?
- Do you think you have a problem?

brilliant suggestion

- The actual sensation of a craving, that gripping desire, only lasts a short time. It may occur frequently but that intense need can clear within moments or minutes.
- Breathe into the craving. Take some deep breaths or stamp your feet, run on the spot or dance about singing. It will dissipate the intensity of the craving.
- If you don't believe it, try it. It helps to break the grip.
- By breathing into the craving you refocus your attention to the part of you that can surf the wave of the craving rather than give into it.

Health

This can include hypertension, chronic heart failure, diabetes, asthma, obesity, irritable bowel syndrome, psoriasis, stress-related conditions, symptoms associated with cancer, arthritis, chronic pain conditions such as fibromyalgia or other health situations. Mindfulness can help with the management of symptoms and increase quality of life around the conditions. It cannot cure or remove them but it can assist with recovery or, if that is not possible, with the way in which you manage yourself, how you approach the difficulty and how you deal with the harshness of the situation.

As an example, stress is implicated in conditions such as hypertension, chronic heart failure, diabetes and IBS. Addressing the stress can help to reduce the severity of the symptoms. Noticing what you are doing and being mindful of your eating, stress levels and use of medication will assist you in managing your illness. A further example is how mindfulness can help symptoms associated with cancer. The main areas where it can assist are with sleep, distress, fear and helping to manage the pain or discomfort thereby improving quality of life. Again, it is important to keep this in perspective, as living with a health condition can range from mild discomfort to excruciating pain and an inevitable end of life.

Mindfulness work can assist, but only assist, in managing emotional and physical discomfort and bring a gentle, caring and open attitude to such difficult times. It cannot remove the illness or the distress but it can offer a kind and generous way to help hold your hand through hard times.

Life tips

- KEEP PERSPECTIVE. There is nothing that throws us off course more quickly than losing perspective on a situation. It may feel like a crisis at the time but it often is more manageable than we believe. If it is a crisis or truly life-changing then know that life is very out of balance at the moment but with time and help some perspective can be regained.

- You are more than your thoughts, disease, emotion or action. They are part of you but not all of you.

- Our thoughts are only thoughts. We don't need to be so attached to them.

- What we feel in our mind is often expressed through our body. If we are stressed, depressed or anxious it sets off a reaction within our brains and bodies: it shows in our health, level of functioning, on our faces and in our interactions and daily tasks.

- By breathing in a focused and balanced way we begin to restore ourselves, rebalance hormonal secretion, increase our immune system and reduce tension. We can balance our minds too and train ourselves to step back from the intensity or distress of whatever is happening.

▶

Life philosophy

- Feeling pain and sadness is part of being a person. Deny suffering and we deny part of our existence as it is an intricate aspect of life as a human being. When we can accept that all things in our lives change, that life is impermanent and transient, we can then release the tightness of our grip on what we have and the desperate grasping for what we want to have.

- Life should change us because neither we nor it stands still. If we hold on to it so tightly in the hope that it will never shift or alter then we are standing in the middle of a tornado expecting not to be moved.

- The more we recognise that life is transient and impermanent and that the only moment we really have is right now the more we can build our resilience and resourcefulness to manage whatever changes occur rather than fire-fight each event. This is what mindfulness can offer us.

- Gently holding what we have in our hands and recognising its existence, whether pleasant or painful, will allow us to see and experience all of it and give it a sense of value.

brilliant insight

Mindfulness is an approach and skill that we all already have but have forgotten to develop. We don't need to go out and find it or buy it. What we need to do is recognise it within ourselves and help it to flourish. In this way, it will become an intrinsic part of your life that will be with you wherever you go.

The concepts and wisdom of mindfulness have been discussed, life issues considered and a selection of mindful practices explained. Now the hard part begins and that is how to continue with it once you've finished the book. The next chapter will give you some ideas on how to do this.

brilliant recap

- A Mindfulness Framework has been provided which you can refer to as a reminder.

- Mindfulness is for good times, ordinary times and difficult times.

- Difficult and harsh situations have been discussed as well as suggestions given to help you manage aspects of them.

- Use the life tips and life philosophy as a lantern in the dark.

Life goes on with or without us. It is up to us to decide how much we want to be part of it.

CHAPTER 8

Keeping it going

This is the final chapter in the book but hopefully not the end of your engagement with the work. As with anything we want to implement and maintain in our lives, we need to continue giving it time, care and attention. Mindfulness is no different.

One of the biggest challenges with any new approach is not how to get it going but how to maintain it. The first step is to recognise that your old ways are familiar. You know what to expect and what to do, even if the feelings are unpleasant, and that is why we revert to our usual way of thinking, feeling and acting. It's a bit like a pair of well-worn slippers. They may have holes in them and be overstretched but they have taken on the shape of your foot.

The more you do it the greater the benefits

The more we do something the more our brains develop a pathway for it. The more we walk along a new track in the forest the more it becomes a footpath clear of branches and undergrowth. The same happens in our brains. When activation takes place between the message centres those brain pathways become more entrenched and the route starts to take shape. If you stop using the route or footpath the undergrowth will take over and the openness of the path will be lost.

We are not too old to learn new tricks. In the past, there was a tendency to believe that the brain stopped developing in one's teens and that whatever was established was there for life. If there was damage in one area it was thought that it couldn't regenerate or that the loss of a function would be permanent. Now, however, we know that the brain continues to develop into a person's twenties. In addition to this, the brain continues to make new connections and create new pathways depending on the input it is given.

▶ brilliant insight

With meditation, it has been found that the more you do it the greater the benefits. Not only do the pathways become stronger but psychologically you are constantly adding to your pool of resilience and developing your resources and skills to manage life.

It may be helpful to restate that mindfulness is not only about managing the hard times but also about giving you more awareness and fulfilment of the good times. It may seem peculiar to think that we don't always make the most of the pleasurable things that happen but we often don't. Our minds are distracted by other events, we wish there was more of the good thing, that it could be even better or we worry that it will disappear in a few minutes or days. We can see a butterfly fluttering past us but it is only when we actually stop long enough to look at the one that has settled on a ledge that we can truly enjoy its beautiful colours and design. We know it will soon fly away but that is what happens. Our lives are much the same. The good comes in for a period of time and we get so much more pleasure from it if we stop and take it in for what it is, even if it changes later down the line.

Day by day

There is no end point with mindfulness. It is ongoing and continually being added to through our life experiences, practice, approach, attitude and interest. Taking an interest in your life and in being mindful is very motivating. It gives you determination to keep at it even when you're feeling tired, low or generally annoyed with the world.

Dipping in and out

The reality is that most people dip in and out of books such as this one. If this book is the first you've read on the subject then it would be helpful if you tried each of the practices, even if only once. It is only through experiencing them that you'll get to know their effects and you could be pleasantly surprised.

brilliant insight

No amount of books will change anything in your life. The struggle is to move from the written word to the doing part – and the only way to do it is to do it.

What this means is that no amount of encouragement will get you to try something new unless you bite the bullet and just do it. Imagine you want to get from one room to another but there is a closed door between them. You can stand there for hours and days hoping the door will open on its own; you can stare at it, shout at it or kick it. Just open the door. That way you'll get to see what is in the room and whether or not you want to be there. You can always walk away and close the door behind you. On the other hand, you may want to keep the door open so that you can enter and leave as you wish, letting the atmosphere and knowledge move between the two rooms.

Whatever you do, do it for you

When you tell yourself that you're taking five or ten minutes for your-self each day because you want to, or you bring some mindfulness into your life in different ways, then you take responsibility for it. If you shift the responsibility to someone else and comment that your wife thinks it's a good idea or your doctor suggested you do it then it has less of a personal value attached to it. By attaching a sense of commitment to what you're doing based on your belief that this is of importance to your life gives it energy.

Be curious and interested in yourself

It makes sense that if you have an interest in something, no matter what, then you'll be more willing to spend time on it, engage with it and even pursue it. The same applies when we take on board that we are our lives and what we think, feel and do is all about us and we can influence it.

Ask yourself how much insight you think you have about the following:

- What motivates you?
- Why do you feel a particular way, such as good about your place in the world or shy?
- What effect did your father have on your self-worth and pride?
- What effect did your mother have on your choice of partner and how you relate to him or her?
- How did your siblings or peers influence your career choice?

These are basic questions that we often don't think to ask. Why do we not ask them? Is it because insight and understanding of oneself is regarded as unnecessary and pointless? Look around at what is happening within the world. If those who have such power and influence over our lives were to be more aware and mindful of their actions and their consequences, would you think differently about it?

It's all relative. When an experience is personal we respond, when it is happening to others we may feel empathy and sadness but we generally don't feel the impact of it in the same way. It is for this reason that one of the ways that you can keep going with mindfulness is to make it personal – to gain more awareness, to improve your relationships, to drink less, to stop smoking, to lower your stress levels, to take more responsibility for your heart condition, to ease the depression, to feel less frightened, to make a choice when you can be in control.

Scepticism is fine

Bringing a sense of curiosity about yourself into your life will raise questions you hadn't previously considered. If you're sceptical about mindfulness and its value, that is appropriate and welcomed as it is through the questioning that you'll start to know whether or not being involved with your life at all these new levels is worth pursuing.

Helping yourself

Mindfulness is not a faddish self-help trick nor is it a magic wand or quick-fix. It would be wonderful to say that by doing this practice or thinking about that comment your life will be transformed. It doesn't work like that and it shouldn't because if it did the chances are it wouldn't stick. Mindfulness is ongoing, one crumb at a time. Each of those crumbs will start to come together to make bigger pieces until one day you realise you have a piece of cake and so it continues.

There will be days, or even weeks and months, where you won't do any formal practice and that is fine. You may be interested this week but not next week and then one day it might pop into your mind and you'll remember a concept and apply it. You may even be feeling angry or in a lot of pain and decide to listen to a piece from the CD.

5 minutes a day is a good start

We spend longer than that fiddling with our phones, checking our emails, making a cup of tea or flipping through a newspaper. On the whole, 5 minutes a day plus 20 minutes three times a week would be a good combination. Some may prefer to do 40 minutes once a week or alternate the practices depending on time and mood.

Find what works for you, though it is worth keeping in mind that random attempts will remain just that, random. That is why getting into the routine of 5 minutes a day keeps it alive in your mind. You can sit quietly in those 5 minutes or do it as part of preparing a meal or eating a meal in silence. You can do it while gardening, watching the birds or sitting on a train.

There is a particular value in sitting quietly for 5 minutes and focusing on your breathing as it is an uninterrupted practice that redirects your attention in a very specific way. That ability to refocus is what you can take into the meeting at work, the difficult conversation with your partner, the first date, the argument with your teenage child, the surge of pain in your hip, the craving for a drink or cigarette, the devastating pain that can come with losing a loved one, when feeling suicidal or desperate from loneliness or when gripped by fear. At each of these times going to your anchor and to that stable centre within yourself will help you rebalance and encourage you to use your resilience to manage whatever it is.

The more you do it the more you will want to do it and the greater the benefits will be both psychologically and neurologically. The way you approach incidents or responses will start to adjust – your attitude to yourself, those harsh and critical remarks you've become so used to and that need for a drink will lessen. You may find yourself when sitting in traffic telling yourself to breathe, or two hours into a business meeting bringing your attention to the soles of your feet.

It will be those everyday difficult things that will remind you of a mindful practice, and when the bigger, sometimes harsher, stuff comes about you'll feel more prepared to brave the storm. It may also be those wonderful moments that you've experienced in an alive and vibrant way that will help to make life seem more bearable because you'll have developed a way of rebalancing yourself in difficult times and of restoring yourself when life feels good.

▶ brilliant insight

There is no end point to all this. You need to work at it on an ongoing basis and if you do you will inevitably feel its benefits.

To end off, this book has offered you a new or different way to approach your life. Change your mindset and you'll move from the arena that sets you up to fail, or to feel inadequate by promising a quick-fix and false hope, to the one that says life is difficult and wonderful, harsh and pleasurable, fearful and exciting. It all co-exists as one.

The aim of mindfulness is to help you to manage all of your experiences not to change your personality or to force philosophies on you. It's about you using what you have in the best way so that it works *for* you and not *against* you.

If you want to promote its caring and profoundly stabilising benefits you need to work at it, encourage it and enjoy it. It will become your internal anchor when the storms hit. It will also become your personal source of kindness and care at all times in life. It builds resilience and resourcefulness, it eases distress and it becomes part of your life framework no matter what is happening. More than that, it becomes part of you and once you start to face its challenges and embrace its wonders you'll return to it on and off over the months or years and eventually feel a great sense of gratitude to have it as part of your life.

Live your life one breath at a time.

References

1 Gardner-Nix, J. (2009). *The mindful solution to pain.* Oakland, CA: New Harbinger Publications, Inc.

2 Nyklicek, I. & Kuijpers, K. F. (2008). Effects of mindfulness-based stress reduction intervention, psychological wellbeing, and quality of life: Is increased mindfulness indeed the mechanism? *Annals of Behavioral Medicine, 35*(3), 331–40.

3 Tang, Y. Y., Ma, Y., Wang, J., Fan, Y., Feng, S., Lu, Q., Sui, D., Rothbart, M. K., Fan, M. & Posner, M. I. (2007). Short-term meditation training improves attention and self-regulation. *Proceedings of the National Academy of Sciences, 104*(43), 17152–6.

4 Kabat-Zinn, J., Massion, A. O., Dristeller, J., Peterson, L. G., Fletcher, K., Pbert, L., Linderking, W. & Santorelli, S. (1992). Effectiveness of a meditation-based stress reduction program in the treatment of anxiety disorders. *American Journal of Psychiatry, 149*(7), 936–43.

5 Miller, J. J., Fletcher, K. & Kabat-Zinn, J. (1995). Three-year follow-up and clinical implications of a mindfulness meditation-based stress reduction intervention in the treatment of anxiety disorders. *General Hospital Psychiatry, 17*(3), 192–200.

6 Goldin, P., Wiveka, R. & Gross, J. (2009). Mindfulness meditation training and self-referential processing in social anxiety disorder: Behavioral and neural effects. *Journal of Cognitive Psychotherapy, 23,* 242–57.

7 Baer, R. A., Smith, G. T., Hopkins, J., Kreitemeyer, J. & Toney, L. (2006). Using self-report assessment methods to explore facets of mindfulness. *Assessment, 13,* 27–45.

8   Davidson, R. J., Kabat-Zinn, J., Schumacher, M., Rosenkranz, D., Muller, D., Santorelli, S. F., Urbanowski, F., Harrington, A., Bonus, K. & Sheridan, J. F. (2003). Alterations in brain and immune function produced by mindfulness meditation. *Psychosomatic Medicine, 65,* 564–70.

9   Davidson, R. J. (2004). Well-being and affective style: Neural substrates and biobehavioral correlates. *Philosophical Transactions of the Royal Society, 359,* 1395–1411.

10   Jain, S., Shapiro, S. L., Swanick, S., Roesch, S. C., Mills, P. J., Bell, I. & Schwartz, G. E. (2007). A randomized controlled trial of mindfulness meditation versus relaxation training: Effects on distress, positive states of mind, rumination, and distraction. *Annals of Behavioral Medicine, 33*(1), 11–21.

11   Cresswell, J. D., Way, B. M., Eisenberger, N. I. & Lieberman, M. D. (2007). Neural correlates of dispositional mindfulness during affect labelling. *Psychosomatic Medicine, 69*(6), 560–5.

12   Deyo, M., Wilson, K. A., Ong, J. & Koopman, C. (2009). Mindfulness and rumination: Does mindfulness training lead to reductions in the ruminative thinking associated with depression? *EXPLORE: The Journal of Science and Healing, 5*(5), 265–71.

13   Segal, Z. V., Williams, M.G., Teasdale, J. D. & Kabat-Zinn, J. (2007). *The mindful way through depression: Freeing yourself from chronic unhappiness.* New York: Guilford.

14   Becker, C. B. & Zayfert, C. (2001). Integrating DBT-based techniques and concepts to facilitate exposure treatment for PTSD. *Cognitive and Behavioral Practice, 8,* 107–22.

15   Cloitre, M., Cohen, L. R. & Koenen, K. C. (2006). *Treating survivors of childhood abuse: Psychotherapy for the interrupted life.* New York: Guilford.

16   Folette, V. M., Palm, K. M. & Pearson, A. N. (2006). Mindfulness and trauma: Implications for treatment. *Journal of Rationale-Emotive and Cognitive-Behavior Therapy, 24*(1), 45–61.

17   Brown, K., Ryan, R. & Cresswell, J. D. (2007). Mindfulness: Theoretical foundations and evidence for its salutary effects. *Psychological Inquiry, 18*(4), 211–37.

18 Siegel, D. J. (2007). *The mindful brain: Reflection and attunement in the cultivation of well-being.* New York: W. W. Norton.

19 Siegel, D. J. (2009). *Mindsight: The new science of personal transformation.* New York: Bantam.

20 Carson, J. W., Carson, K. M., Gill, K. M. & Baucom, D. H. (2006). Mindfulness-based relationship enhancement (MBRE) in couples. In R. A. Baer (ed.), *Mindfulness-based treatment approaches: Clinicians' guide to evidence base and applications* (pp. 309–29).

21 Blake, C. (2010). *The joy of mindful sex: Be in the moment and enrich your lovemaking.* Lewes: Ivy Press.

22 Goldmeier, D. & Mears, A. J. (2010). Meditation: A review of its use in Western medicine and, in particular, its role in the management of sexual dysfunction. *Current Psychiatry Reviews, 6*(1), 11–14.

23 Parks, G. A., Anderson, B. K. & Marlatt, G. A. (2001). *Interpersonal handbook of alcohol dependence and problems.* New York: John Wiley.

24 Bowen, S., Witkiewitz, K., Dillworth, T. M., Chawla, N., Simpson, T., Ostafin, B., *et al.* (2006). Mindfulness meditation and substance use in an incarcerated population. *Psychology of Addictive Behaviors, 20*(3), 343–47.

25 Brefczynski-Lewis, J. A., Lutz, A., Schaefer, H. S., Levinson, D. B. & Davidson, R. J. (2007). Neural correlates of attentional expertise in long-term meditation practitioners. *Proceedings of the National Academy of Sciences, 104*(27), 11483–88.

26 Witkiewitz, K. & Bowen, S. (2010). Depression, craving and substance use following a randomized trial of mindfulness-based relapse prevention. *Journal of Consulting and Clinical Psychology, 78*(3), 362–74.

27 Davis, J. M. (2007). A pilot study on mindfulness-based stress reduction for smokers. *BMC Complementary and Alternative Medicine, 7*, 2.

28 Kristeller, J. L., Baer, R. A. & Quillan-Wolver, R. (2006). Mindfulness based approaches to eating disorders. In R. A. Baer (ed.), *Mindfulness-based treatment approaches: Clinician's guide to evidence base and applications* (pp. 75–93).

29 Merkes, M. (2010). Mindfulness-based stress reduction for people with chronic disease. *Australian Journal of Primary Health, 16*(3), 200–10.

30 Kabat-Zinn, J., Wheeler, E., Light, T., Skillings, A., Scharf, M., Cropley, T., Hosmer, D. & Bernhard, J. (1998). Influence of a mindfulness meditation-based stress reduction intervention on rates of skin clearing in patients with moderate to severe psoriasis undergoing phototherapy (UVB) and photochemotherapy (PUVB). *Psychosomatic Medicine, 60*(5), 625–32.

31 Winbush, N. Y., Gross, C. R. & Kreitzer, M. J. (2007). The effects of mindfulness-based stress reduction on sleep disturbance: A systematic review. *Explore(NY), 3*(6), 585–91.

32 Britton, W. B., Bootzin, R. R., Cousins, J. C., Haslwer, B. P., Peck, T. & Shapiro, S. L. (2010). The contribution of mindfulness practice to a multicomponent behavioural sleep intervention following substance abuse treatment in adolescents: A treatment-development study. *Substance Abuse, 31*(2), 86–97.

33 Cresswell, J. D., Myers, H. F., Cole, S. W. & Irwin, M. R. (2009). Mindfulness meditation training effects on CD4+ T lymphocytes in HIV-1 infected adults: A small randomized controlled trial. *Brain, Behavior, and Immunity, 23*(2), 184–8.

34 Jam, S., Imani, A. H., Foroughi, M., Seyed Alinaghi, S., Koochak, H. E. & Mohraz, M. (2010). The effects of mindfulness-based stress reduction (MBSR) program in Iranian HIVAIDS patients: A pilot study. *Acta Medica Iranica, 48*(2), 101–6.

35 Carlson, L., Speca, M., Faris, P. & Patel, K. (2007). One year pre-post intervention follow-up of psychological, immune, endocrine and blood pressure outcomes of mindfulness-based stress reduction (MBSR) in breast and prostate cancer outpatients. *Brain, Behavior, and Immunity, 21*(8), 1038–49.

36 Witek-Janusek, L., Albuquerque, K., Chroniak, K. R., Chroniak, C., Durazo-Arvizu, R. & Mathews, H. L. (2008). Effect of mindfulness-based stress reduction on immune function, quality of life, and coping in women newly diagnosed with early stage breast cancer. *Brain, Behavior, and Immunity, 22*(6), 969–81.

37 Morone, N. E., Greco, C. M. & Weiner, D. K. (2008). Mindfulness meditation for the treatment of chronic lower back pain in older adults: A randomized controlled study. *Pain, 134*(3), 310–19.

38 Schmidt, S., Grossman, P., Schwarzer, B., Jena, S., Naumann, J. & Walach, H. (2011). Treating fibromyalgia with mindfulness-based stress reduction: Results from a 3-armed randomized controlled trial. *Pain, 152*, 361–9.

39 Sephton, S. E., Salmon, P., Weissbecker, I., Ulmer, C., Floyd, A., Hoover, K. & Studts, J. L. (2007). Mindfulness meditation alleviates depressive symptoms in women with fibromyalgia: Results of a randomized clinical trial. *Arthritis and Rheumatism, 57*(1), 77–85.

40 Pradhan, E., Baumgarten, M., Langenberg, P., Handwerger, B., Kaplin Gilpin, A., Magyari, T., Hochberg, M. C. & Berman, B. M. (2007). Effect of mindfulness-based stress reduction in rheumatoid arthritis patients. *Arthritis and Rheumatism, 57*(7), 1134–42.

41 Tacon, A. M., McComb, J., Caldera, Y. & Randolph, P. (2003). Mindfulness meditation, anxiety reduction, and heart disease: A pilot study. *Complementary and Alternative Therapies, 26*(1), 25–33.

42 Bauer-Wu, S., Sullivan, A. M., Rosenbaum, E., Ott, M. J., Powell, M., McLoughlin, M. & Healey, M. W. (2008). Facing the challenges of hematopoietic stem cell transplantation with mindfulness meditation: A pilot study. *Integrative Cancer Therapies, 7*(2), 62–9.

43 Speca, M., Carlson, L. E., Goodey, E. & Angen, M. (2000). A randomized, wait-list controlled clinical trial: The effect of a mindfulness meditation-based stress reduction program on mood and symptoms of stress in cancer outpatients. *Psychosomatic Medicine, 62*, 613–22.

44 Carlson, L. E. & Garland, S. N. (2005). Impact of mindfulness-based stress reduction (MBSR) on sleep, mood, stress, and fatigue symptoms in cancer outpatients. *International Journal of Behavioral Medicine, 12*(4), 278–85.

45 Shapiro, S. L., Bootzin, R. R., Figueredo, A. J., Lopez, A. M. & Schwartz, G. E. (2003). The efficacy of mindfulness-based stress reduction in the treatment of sleep disturbance in women with

breast cancer: An exploratory study. *Journal of Psychosomatic Research, 54,* 85–91.

46 Carlson, L. E., Speca, M., Patel, K. D. & Goodey, E. (2004). Mindfulness-based stress reduction in relation to quality of life, mood, symptoms of stress and levels of cortisol, dehydroepiandros-terone sulphate (DHEAS) and melatonin in breast and prostate cancer outpatients. *Psychoneuroendocrinology, 29*(4), 448–74.

47 Lazar, S. W., Kerr, C. E., Wasserman, R. H., Gray, J. R., Greve, D. N., Treadway, M. T. *et al.* (2005). Meditation experience is associated with increased cortical thickness. *NeuroReport, 16*(17), 1893–97.

48 Holzel, B. K., Ott, U., Gard, T., Hempel, H., Weygandt, M., Morgen, K. & Vaitl, D. (2008). Investigation of mindfulness meditation practitioners with voxel-based morphometry. *Social, Cognitive and Affective Neuroscience, 3,* 55–61.

49 Lewis, M. D. & Todd, R. M. (2007). The self-regulatory brain: Cortical-subcortical feedback and the development of intelligent action. *Cognitive Development, 22,* 406–30.

50 Jha, P., Krompinger, J. & Baime, M. J. (2007). Mindfulness training modifies subsystems of attention. *Cognitive, Affective, and Behavioral Neuroscience, 7*(2), 109–19.

51 Tang, Y. Y., Lu, Q., Geng, X., Stein, E. A., Yang, Y. & Posner, M. I. (2010). Short-term meditation includes white matter changes in the anterior cirgulate. *Proceedings of the National Academy of Sciences, 107*(35), 15649–52.

52 Pbert, L., Madison, J. M., Druker, S., Olendzki, N., Magner, R., Reed, G., Allison, J. & Carmody, J. (2011). Effect of mindfulness training on asthma quality of life and lung function: A randomised controlled trial. Thorax doi:10.1136/thoraxjnl-2011-200253.

53 Rezek, C. A. (2010). *Life happens: Waking up to yourself and your life in a mindful way.* London: Leachcroft.

Further reading

Chodron, P. (1997). *When things fall apart.* Boston: Shambala.

Gunaratana, B. H. (2002). *Mindfulness in plain English.* Boston: Wisdom.

Kabat-Zinn, J. & Davidson, R. J. (eds.) (2011). *The mind's own physician: A scientific dialogue with the Dalai Lama on the healing power of meditation.* Oakland, CA: New Harbinger Publications, Inc.

Kornfield, J. (1993). *A path with heart.* New York: Bantam.

Nhat Hahn, T. (1996). *The miracle of mindfulness.*

Rezek, C. A. (2010). *Life happens: Waking up to yourself and your life in a mindful way.* London: Leachcroft.

Santorelli, S. (1999). *Heal thyself: Lessons in mindfulness in medicine.* New York: Three Rivers Press.

Siegel, D. J. (2009). *Mindsight: The new science of personal transformation.* New York: Bantam.

Resources

www.dharmaseed.org An excellent site with extensive material on mindfulness and Buddhist concepts.

www.gaiahouse.co.uk A centre in the UK. It also provides resource information.

www.mindandlife.org Mind and Life Institute (the Dalai Lama is closely associated with this centre).

www.spiritrock.com A well-known centre in the USA. It also provides resource information.

Guided meditations

Further guided meditations are provided in CD format with the book *Life Happens: Waking up to your life in a mindful way* by the author, or can be downloaded in MP3 format at www.lifehappens-mindfulness. com where further information on the author's work is available.

Index